BAHRAIN
ISLAND HERITAGE

Shirley Kay

This edition has been extensively revised and updated,
with new photographs, by Rosalind Ingrams.

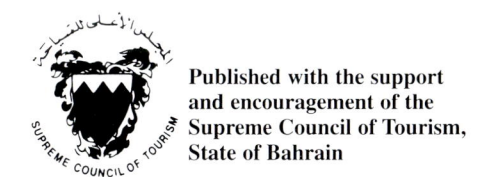

Published with the support
and encouragement of the
Supreme Council of Tourism,
State of Bahrain

MOTIVATE
PUBLISHING

Dedicated to the late Mohamed Akbar Ali Reza
and family, our close friends for more than 20 years,
and to Toby Kay who was born here.

Published by
Motivate Publishing

Dubai: PO Box 2331, Dubai, UAE
Tel: 04 824060, Fax: 04 824436
E-mail: motivate@emirates.net.ae

Abu Dhabi: PO Box 43072, Abu Dhabi, UAE
Tel: 02 271666, Fax: 02 271888

London: Macmillan House, 96 Kensington High Street London W8 4SG.
Tel: 0171 937 7733/0171 937 4024, Fax: 0171 937 7293

Directors:
Obaid Humaid Al Tayer
Ian Fairservice

First published 1989
Revised edition 1993
New edition 1998
Revisions for the 1998 edition by Rosalind Ingrams

© **Motivate Publishing 1989, 1993 and 1998**

All rights reserved. No part of this publication may be
reproduced in any material form (including photocopying
or storing in any medium by electronic means) without the
written permission of the copyright holder. Applications for the
copyright holder's written permission to reproduce any part
of this publication should be addressed to the publishers.
In accordance with the International Copyright Act 1956
or the UAE Federal Copyright Law No 40 of 1992,
any person acting in contravention of this copyright
will be liable to criminal prosecution and
civil claims for damages.

ISBN 1 86063 049 9

British Library Cataloguing-in-Publication Data.
A catalogue record for this book is available
from the British Library.

Printed by Emirates Printing Press, Dubai

His Highness Shaikh Isa bin Salman Al Khalifa
The Amir of the State of Bahrain

FOREWORD

I am pleased to introduce this new edition of Shirley Kay's highly informative and enjoyable book 'Bahrain: Island Heritage'. The new edition contains significant additions and updated information, as well as more recent photographs of Bahrain, such as those of the new Muharraq Bridge, the Manama coastline and Zallaq.

The book successfully conveys to the reader a sense of Bahrain's rich heritage, modernisation and development. It introduces the general reader to the many varied facets of Bahraini life and civilisation, the traditional and the modern, and to Bahrain's industries, architecture and the factors that stimulate its growing tourism industry. Thus the reader is made to appreciate the fascinating diversity and richness of a small country like Bahrain.

Much of Bahrain's progress is due to the fact that it has been blessed with stability and security. It has been ruled by the Al Khalifas for more than 200 years, and under the guidance and wise leadership of its present Amir, HH Shaikh Isa bin Salman Al Khalifa, Bahrain has greatly developed in many fields, including health, education, housing, roads and transport, industry, banking and financial services, the expansion and construction of power desalination plants, tourism and the media.

This book has been written by someone who has clearly known and loved Bahrain. I greatly appreciate the author's efforts in updating the book and thank Motivate Publishing for producing this new edition.

Bahrain has always looked out to the world, and Bahrainis have interacted with other peoples and civilisations for thousands of years. This has certainly contributed to the country's liberal climate and openness, and to the welcome and hospitality which Bahrainis are accustomed to and glad to extend to all visitors.

Mohammad Ebrahim Al-Mutawa
Minister of Cabinet Affairs and Information

Front and back cover and contents page photography by Rosalind Ingrams

CONTENTS

The Land and the People	6
The Burial Mounds	14
A Seafaring Nation	24
A Sense of Style	32
Manama the Capital	40
Muharraq Island	52
The North Coast Green Belt	60
The West Coast	70
Townships of the Centre	80
The Industrial East Coast	90
Mountain and Mirage	98
Tourism and Hotels	106
Index	114

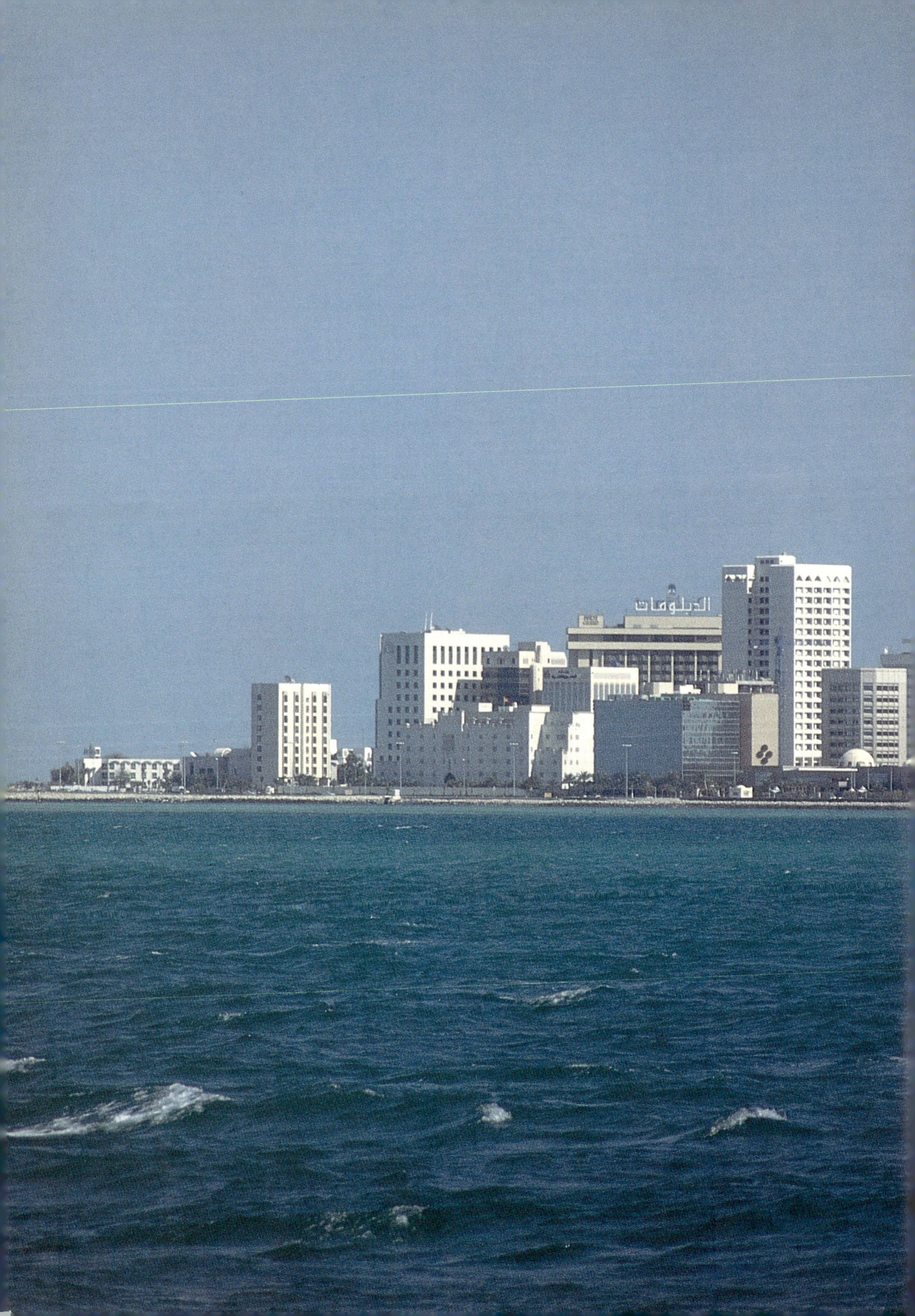

Chapter 1

THE LAND AND THE PEOPLE

"The King of Dilmun, whose abode lies like a fish, 30 double hours away in the midst of the sea of the rising sun, heard of my might and sent gifts," recorded King Sargon of Akkad (reigned 2334-2279 BC).

This is one of the oldest geographical descriptions of Bahrain (called Dilmun or Tilmun in ancient times), whose islands do indeed seem to float in the warm shallow seas of the Gulf. They lie not far from the shores of Saudi Arabia and Qatar, a shoal of sandbanks and islands pushing up above the aquamarine waters, some only to submerge again at high tide. So shallow is the sea around them that a man can wade out, half a kilometre or so, with the water still only up to his knees.

Where an island emerges definitively from the water, however, it fast loses its sandbank appearance. For the extraordinary thing about the islands of Bahrain, the one factor which has distinguished them from the areas around them, is that they have always enjoyed abundant sweet water.

Today the Bahrain archipelago consists of 33 islands, of which the larger ones are green, supporting lush palm groves and gardens. The water which nourishes these plantations emerges from the ground in a number of springs, bubbling up in clear pools.

Even stranger, sweet water emerges in places from the sea bed and can be collected by a man swimming down to the source with a leather bag. The name Bahrain, which means 'two seas', is thought to refer to these two different waters: the salt water of the Gulf and the sweet water below it.

Scientists have long debated the source of so much sweet water in so arid a region. The most likely explanation seems to be that it is an aquifer of ancient, geological water, flowing like an underground river from beneath the Arabian Peninsula.

Modern Manama from the sea: the diplomatic and financial quarter.

BAHRAIN ISLAND

The main island of the group bears the name of the whole, Bahrain. It covers 590 of the country's total 706.5 square kilometres area. The island is 48 kilometres long from north to south, and 16 kilometres at the widest point from east to west. Originally this was a great dome of limestone rock, pushed up by ancient pressures, but since that time it has eroded almost away. This explains the strange configuration of the island, which consists of a raised rocky ridge running all around a central depression, to which it drops in abrupt cliffs, some 20 metres high.

From the centre of the depression rises the island's one high point, Jebel Dukhan (Smoky Mountain), 122.4 metres above sea level. It is an arid place of crumbling, sandy-coloured rock, barren like the rest of the depression and the rim rock around it.

Surrounding the rim rock, however, is a coastal plain of great fertility. To the west, north and east of this raised ridge, palm groves run down to the sea; only in the south is the plain beyond the ridge, barren desert and salt flats.

The inhabitants of the island have always made their homes around the shores, where they could cultivate the land and exploit the rich fisheries of the sea beyond. In the northern part of the island there were also settlements some way inland, as far south as the palm tree could be cultivated. But for the most part, towns and villages were built near the beach.

The seafront, then, became the most populous and desirable location, but the waters lapping the beach were shallow. So in recent years an extensive programme of land reclamation has taken place. Originally soil was brought from inland and dumped to fill the shallows. Today, however, a more economical method has been found: when channels are dredged through the shallows, the spoil is used to make new land and this sea sludge hardens in time almost to the quality of rock.

Thus the coastline of the islands has changed dramatically over the past two decades, particularly around the towns of Manama and Muharraq. The old coastline can be traced today only by the abrupt edge of the palm groves, now some way inland, or by a line of old houses, once sited on the beach. The new land is devoted to modern buildings, like those of the diplomatic quarter of Manama, or to corniche highways.

Perhaps the most significant use of these land-building skills has been the construction of the causeway linking Bahrain with Saudi Arabia. Throughout its known history, spanning 5,000 years or more, Bahrain had been an island. True, it was politically closely linked with the Arabian Peninsula, particularly in the earliest

Cliffs of the rim rock which encircles the central depression.

times when Dilmun was the name for the islands and much of the Saudi coastline as well. But now there is a physical link too, a road link running over causeways and bridges, opened in 1986 – the longest such link in the world.

Perhaps, in the end, this will not make much difference to the character of the place. For Bahrain was never isolated by the surrounding seas, never particularly insular in nature. Her people always launched their vessels with confidence across the waters, and from the earliest times drew their main prosperity from the seas.

In the earliest times of which there is any record, more than 4,000 years ago, the Bahrainis (or men of Dilmun, as they were then called) made a living, and a good one, from maritime trade. Their ships plied the seas between Pakistan, Oman and Iraq, carrying the lucrative trade of the ancient world, and landing at their capital on the north coast to take their transit dues.

In later years prosperity came from pearling. In the summer months the *dhows* sailed out to the oyster banks; the divers, weighted down with stones, dropped to the sea bed to cull the promising oyster shells. This, too, was an ancient occupation. Pliny, writing almost 2,000 years ago, remarked: "The island of Tylos (Bahrain again) is famous for the vast number of its pearls." It was famous for their quality, too, said to be among the best in the world.

The pearl trade, however, died a sudden death in the 1930s through a combination of the world slump and the introduction of Japanese cultured pearls. Bahrain's future would have been bleak, had relief not come from a quite different direction.

Sculptured limestone rocks of the central depression were the site of Stone Age flint mines.

OIL IN BAHRAIN

Oil, which for the past half-century has been the mainstay of Bahrain's economy, was not unknown in the island in the distant past. Bitumen-covered palm-frond baskets and beakers are found in the ancient tombs. But the inhabitants found no other use for this sticky black substance than to make impermeable baskets, and perhaps to caulk their boats. To a geologist's eye, however, the island had promise. The strange, eroded dome which was the island of Bahrain was what geologists call an anticline, a rock layer forced up in a dome which should have a cavern beneath it. Such caverns are known often to serve as reservoirs in which oil, over the ages, may collect.

In the early 1920s an energetic New Zealander, Major Frank Holmes, was busy collecting concessions to prospect for oil in the Gulf. Although his syndicate had no means of drilling itself, he actually obtained

The oil refinery forms a backdrop to fishermen working in the shallows, with an aluminium cable car swinging overhead.

BAHRAIN – ISLAND HERITAGE

Oil tanker anchored off the Bahrain shores.

Oil pipelines snake across the desert and criss-cross the island.

concessions in Saudi Arabia, the Kuwait neutral zone, and on Bahrain.

His concession for Bahrain, granted in 1925, was valid only for two years, but he failed to convince any British oil company to drill there. Just before the concession ran out, however, he persuaded Standard Oil of California to take it, and they set up a subsidiary, BAPCO (registered in Canada to comply with the ruling that it must be a British company), to prospect and exploit the area.

At that time no oil was known in the Gulf or the Arabian Peninsula. Drilling in Bahrain was a shot in the dark, and only Frank Holmes really had faith in the project. Five years were to pass before suddenly, in 1932, his faith was justified; oil gushed from a trial well at the foot of Jebel Dukhan. This was the first oil struck in Arabia. The success in Bahrain inspired renewed efforts elsewhere in the Gulf and oil was soon found in Kuwait, Qatar and Saudi Arabia, but just too late to be extensively developed before World War Two cast a pall on activities there. So Bahrain had a head start over its neighbours in the oil industry. Although the Bahrain wells were never to be big producers by Gulf standards, this start made a significant difference to life on the islands.

A refinery was built by 1937 to process Bahrain's oil. Later it was greatly expanded to become at the time one of the largest refineries outside the USA, fed by oil from Saudi Arabia brought from 1945 onwards through a pipeline under the sea. The refinery became the island's major source of employment.

Schoolboys with their teacher on a visit to the National Museum.

Although the production of the Bahrain field is small for the region, the refinery processes a much greater quantity, much of it coming from Saudi Arabia. By 1980 the country also started to exploit its large reserves of natural gas. By the end of the decade production of natural gas rose to some 700 million cubic feet a day.

HEALTH AND EDUCATION

The oil income arrived at a critical period, when revenue from pearling was suddenly showing a sharp decline. In the first half of the century pearls had given Bahrain considerable prosperity, relative to the region as a whole.

This prosperity led very early on to developments in health and education which provided a framework within which oil wealth could be rapidly and effectively used.

The first hospital was opened in Bahrain by the American Mission in 1902 and is still popular today. When oil wealth became available in the 1930s, a government hospital was built in Manama, and opened in 1940. The large Sulmaniya Hospital was opened in 1958 and has been considerably enlarged over the years since then.

Perhaps even more vital to the development of the country was the early opening of schools there. The first boys' school was started, partly by public subscription, in Muharraq in 1919. This was followed a few years later by a second school for boys in Manama, and by 1937 there were three town schools and five village schools in the islands.

The girls were not forgotten in this early introduction of education. The first girls' school was opened in the late 1920s, with the support of the Ruler and of one of the leading pearl merchants, Muhammad Zainal Ali Reza. The girls soon proved their worth as scholars and by the mid-1950s were taking more prizes in state exams than the boys.

Children's health and education have advanced rapidly in Bahrain.

Prestigious buildings of the Bahrain University.

Today there are more than 170 schools in the islands, with some 100,000 students. Bahrain also has two universities. The older of these, the Bahrain University at Hamad Town, resulted from the amalgamation in 1986 of the Gulf Technical College founded back in the 1960s, and the Gulf University College.

Its magnificent modern campus, immediately to the south of Hamad Town, was opened in 1988 for the ambitious project of an Arabian Gulf University, to be financed by the GCC countries and Iraq. This post-graduate foundation got off to a slow start; it has now been removed to the former premises of the Bahrain University at Isa Town.

The Arabian Gulf University has a College of Applied Science, specialising in arid zone studies and biotechnology, and a College of Education. It also runs the College of Medicine at Sulmaniya, which had been started in the early 1980s and takes students through from pre-medical training to final qualification as doctors.

A Confident People

With a school system now more than 70 years old, Bahrain had a head start over the rest of the region as a source of educated professional people. The effects of widespread education are noticeable also in the creation of an open, relaxed and confident society.

Bahraini women, whose schooling is nearly as long established as that of the men, play an active role at all levels of the economy. Since the 1960s they have held jobs in all the professions, and many are involved in the country's commerce, as owners of shops and boutiques. Their sophisticated dress sense brings a touch of the Faubourg St Honoré into Bahraini salons.

Bahrain's easy, friendly society has actually been forged by people of very varied origins. In the past the islands changed hands many times: Persians, Portuguese, Arabs from the mainland, and Omanis made themselves

Schoolgirls are diligent students.

masters there in turn. But stability and prosperity have been brought to Bahrain over the past two centuries by the Al Khalifa family who have ruled the islands since 1783.

The Al Khalifas are of the 'Utub tribe, members of the great north Arabian tribal federation of Anaiza. They are related to the Al Sabahs of Kuwait and moved south from there more than two centuries ago, to Zubara in Qatar. But in 1782 they were attacked by the Ruler of Bahrain; in response, the following year, Shaikh Ahmad Al Khalifa captured the islands of Bahrain and established a stable dynasty there.

In 1869 the British helped to establish the 21-year-old Isa bin Ali Al Khalifa as Ruler, against rival family claims. Shaikh Isa died in 1932, having presided over one of the longest and most stable periods in Bahrain's history. The British had signed treaties of protection with Bahrain and others in the Gulf in 1820 and again in 1860. These were to counter slave traffic and piracy, and later to resist Turkish and German ambitions eastwards. The Bahraini-British defensive agreement was formally dissolved in 1971.

When the Al Khalifas first came to Bahrain the population of the island was easily contained in a number of little villages around the coast and in the northern part of the island, and in two small towns. This was still the case up to a generation ago, when the population really began to soar.

In a census taken in 1950 there were found to be 110,000 people in Bahrain, more than 90,000 of them Bahrainis. By the 1981 census there were 351,000 inhabitants and by 1991 almost half a million. The figure continues to rise.

This rapid expansion of population has greatly altered the aspect of the islands over the past few decades. Areas which were formerly palm groves or desert are now covered with villas, estates and new towns, so that much of the northern and central parts of the island are now urbanised. Even so there is still a pressing demand for more low-cost housing, and as a result, the Government is considering a further development on the lines of Isa and Hamad towns.

These vast building programmes have inevitably disturbed some of the country's extensive archaeological heritage. At the same time, however, they have given the incentive for widespread rescue 'digs' which have brought to light rich collections of ancient artefacts, as well as helping to solve the mystery of Bahrain's huge fields of burial mounds.

A magnificent new museum was opened in Manama in 1988 to house what must be the richest collection of antiquities in Arabia. This purpose-built, well-documented museum gives the most impressive picture of the region's past available anywhere in the Gulf.

Since the accession of Shaikh Isa bin Salman Al Khalifa in 1961, Bahrain has progressed immensely.

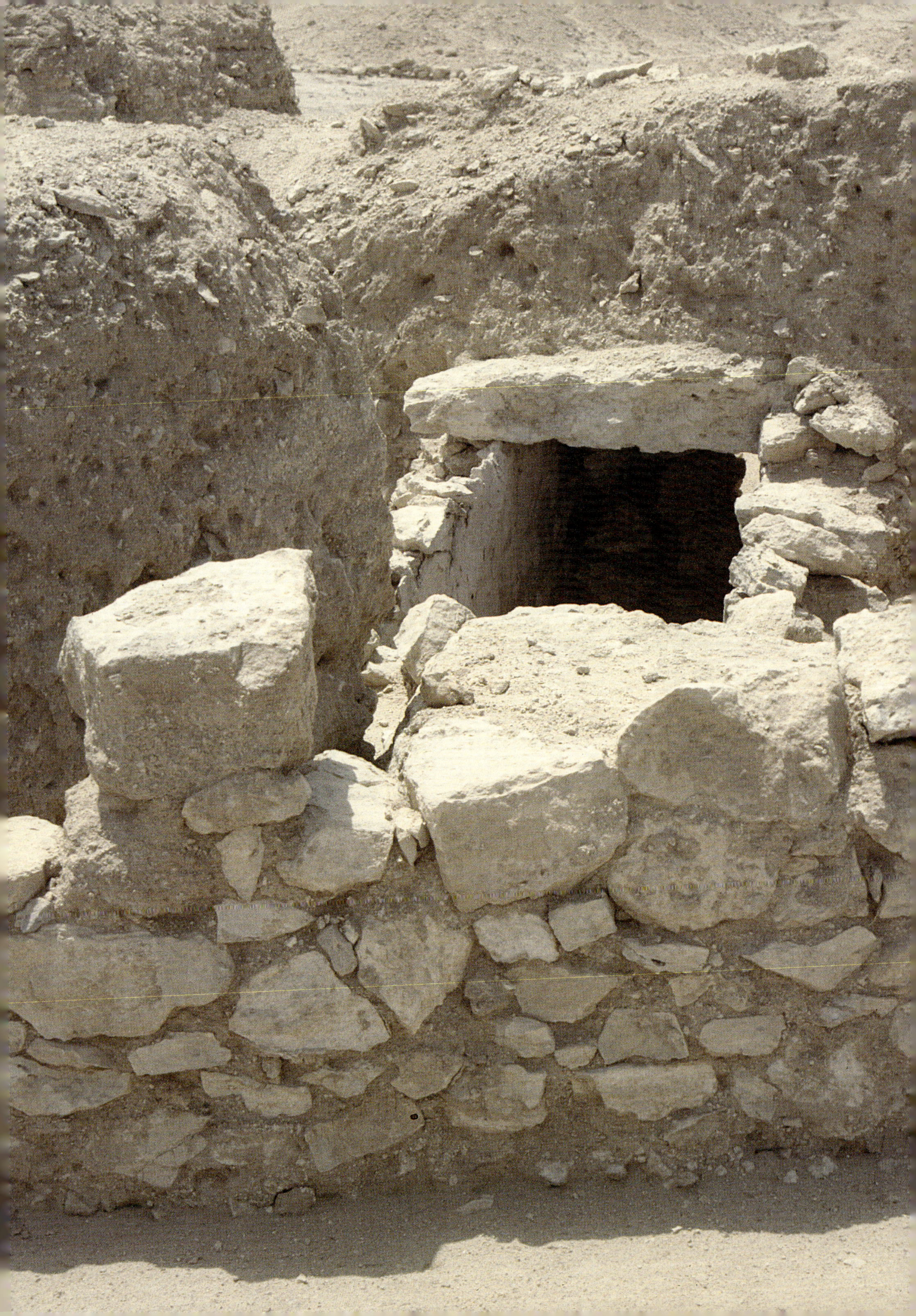

An excavated burial mound showing the stone-built grave and the surrounding ring wall.

Chapter 2

THE BURIAL MOUNDS

Before the huge recent building programmes, and resultant clearing of many mounds, the most unforgettable impression a visitor would have taken away would have been of the enormous fields of ancient burials: a "vast sea of sepulchral mounds" as Theodore Bent, a traveller in the 19th century, described them. These barren mounds crowd close together on the flanks of the rim rock, extending as far as the eye can see. Indeed, since they often stand higher than a man, one can easily walk in among them only to realise that it is far from easy to find the way out again.

On the arid slopes of the northern part of the island are thousands of these tumuli, the largest ancient necropolis in the world. In the early 1980s there were estimated to be 170,000 burial mounds in Bahrain, covering some 30 square kilometres of land, or five per cent of the total island. Since then the numbers have diminished with extensive modern development, but hundreds of mounds have been examined in rescue excavations.

Unfortunately the archaeologists are not the first to have entered these tombs. Almost all of the mounds show a slight dip at the top, or in the west side, a dimple which betrays the entrance of robbers in ancient times. Sometimes a scatter of broken pottery pressed into the soil near the mound shows where the ancient tomb robbers discarded pottery they found of little interest; they were seeking metal, a rare and valuable commodity in those early times.

That the burial mounds are very ancient has long been realised. Today's excavations have shown that most of them were built between about 2225 BC and 1600 BC, with other groups of more shapeless, spreading mounds dating from about 300 BC until the centuries before Islam. By far the largest number, however, were built over a period of four or five centuries, around 4,000 years ago.

Such huge ancient cemeteries on so small an island led early researchers to suggest that Bahrain must have served

An excavated burial mound showing the stone-built grave and the surrounding ring wall.

15

as a cemetery island, with bodies being brought from the mainland for burial. However, recent archaeological research has shown that Bahrain's own people could have accounted for these tombs themselves, if all were buried that way; a population of 18,000, with the life expectancy of the time (between 30 and 50 years), would have needed 150,000 tombs in 250 years.

Sometimes, though, a child's grave was inserted into the edge of the mound as well. The graves were the same for both women and men, and the dead were accompanied by objects of everyday life – food (animal bones and date skins have been found), pots, weapons such as spear-heads, daggers, swords and arrowheads for men, beads for women, occasionally an ostrich eggshell used as a beaker, small pieces of ivory inlay or figurines, a bone bowl, or a tiny trace of gold. Since virtually all the mounds have been robbed the latter finds are rare.

In the early 1980s, however, an ancient cemetery of a rather different type was discovered to the south of Sar, on the line of the new highway to the Saudi Causeway. Here the ground was marked by low bumps rather than individual mounds, and these were found to cover hundreds of closely packed graves, the ring wall around each tomb adjoining that of the next, like some giant honeycomb. These were the graves of the poorer people. The funerary offerings: pottery, beads, seals,

Above: The most common type of jar found in the burial mounds. Below: Interior of the temple at Sar, with crescent-shaped backs to altars.

THE BURIAL MOUNDS

and so forth, showed the graves to be of the same period as the Barbar temple, about 2200 to 1750 BC (see page 62, chapter 7).

Study of the skeletons in Bahrain's ancient graves has shown that the people were fit and strong. The men stood 1.7 metres high on average, the women a little less, and many reached an age of up to 50 years, a good age for those times. They suffered a good deal from tooth decay, a consequence of the quantities of dates which they ate as a staple of their diet.

THE LAND OF DILMUN

Although few ancient inscriptions have been found in Bahrain, quite a lot is known about the region from the cuneiform tablets of the Sumerians and the Assyrians, in the land that is now Iraq, known as Mesopotamia in antiquity. The Sumerians and the Egyptians, at almost the same time, developed the world's first high civilisations. Trading accounts from Sumeria from as far back as the third millennium BC mention a land called Dilmun, or Tilmun, as a trading partner on the route to the south and east. Timber from India and copper from Oman were the principal goods sent to Iraq. Dilmun meant more than the islands of Bahrain today. Dilmun was a region that

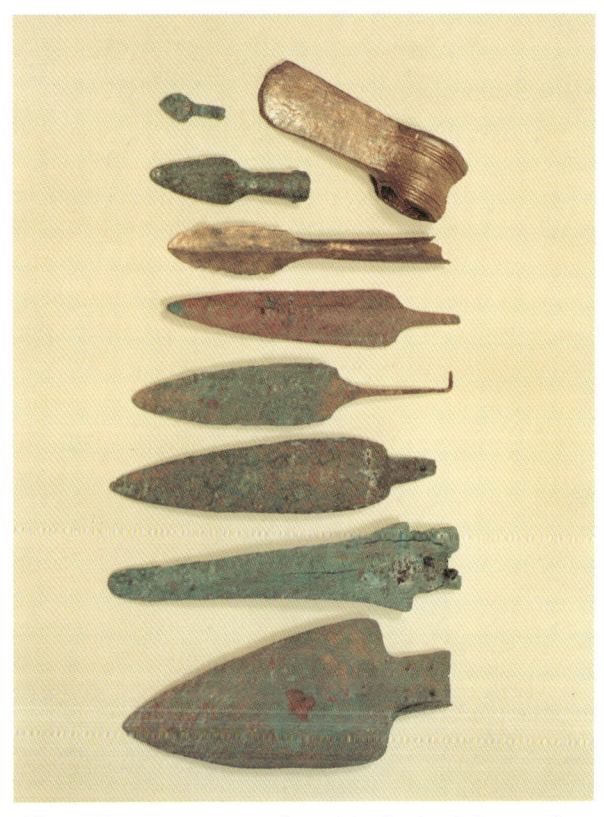

Above: Bronze weapons found in the burial mounds. Below: A Bahraini archaeologist excavates the skeleton of a man buried some 2,000 years ago.

included the Al Hasa strip of the eastern coast of present-day Saudi Arabia, running almost as far north as Kuwait, and including Failaka Island.

In 1878 a short cuneiform inscription was found in Bahrain itself, carved on a foot-shaped black stone which was set into the wall of an old mosque in Bilad al Qadim. It read "Palace of Rimum, servant of the god Inzak, man of the tribe of Agarum". Inzak was known to be the special god of Dilmun, but as yet the whereabouts of Dilmun had not been discovered. The discovery of this inscription on the island set scholars on the quest for Dilmun.

Dilmun in the cuneiform texts was not only a merchant state. It was a land of myth and legend, a paradise land connected with some of the oldest stories known to mankind. A Sumerian poem ran:

"The land of Dilmun is holy
the land of Dilmun is pure
the land of Dilmun is clean...
the lion kills not, the wolf
snatches not the lamb..."

The Sumerians also wrote the first version of the great flood, Noah's flood to most people. The Sumerian survivor was not called Noah, but Ziusudra.

"Anu and Enlil (the gods) cherished Ziusudra, life like a god they gave him... then Ziusudra, the king, in the land of the crossing, the land of Dilmun, the place where the sun rises, they caused to dwell."

Another Sumerian legend told how the hero Gilgamesh, the semi-mythical king of Uruk, visited Ziusudra in search of immortality. He was told that the flower of immortality lay at the bottom of the sea and that he should attach stones to his feet (as pearl-divers did) and swim down to get it. He "opened the sluices so that a sweet-water current might carry him out to the deepest channel". Gilgamesh succeeded in bringing up the flower (thought by some to mean a pearl) and resolved to take it back to Uruk and give it to the old men to eat. "Its name shall be 'The Old Men Shall Be Young Again' and at last I shall eat it myself and have back all my lost youth." But during the return journey Gilgamesh stops to bathe in a pool of cool water and a snake comes out of the water and steals away the flower. Gilgamesh laments bitterly when he discovers the loss: "Already the stream has carried it 20 leagues back to the channels where I found it." This passage seems to show that a pattern of underwater fresh springs and currents was well-known in ancient times.

In 1953 a team of Danish archaeologists arrived to explore the island hoping to find something different from the multitude of graves. They started to dig among the low sand dunes of the north coast at a place near Diraz where a ring of well-cut stones lay scattered on the surface. Local legend claimed that this had been the well of Umm as Sejour, destroyed as a punishment to the islanders in the early centuries of Islam (see chapter 7). The excavation indeed revealed a well-made flight of plastered stone steps leading to a little stone-lined well chamber below, and two headless stone statues of rams. Recently another flight of steps has been uncovered. There was also pottery of a kind they had never seen before; pottery of which they were to find much more in another mound nearby.

The Danes had also begun to work on a large mound near the village of Barbar. This mound revealed many well-cut stones: the diggers were able to trace huge walls and staircases, a stone-flagged pavement, and again, a well. The well was clearly of ritual significance (many offerings were found in it) and scholars have been quick to link it to the name of Enki, or Ea, the Sumerian god of wisdom. He is also the god of the sweet waters under the earth and the sea, the abyss (*absu* in Sumerian).

At the top of the Barbar mound the archaeologists found remains of a stone bench, an altar, and an offerings pit in which, among other things, was a little copper statuette of a suppliant. An alabaster vase was also found, and a beautiful little head of a bull cast in copper, which has become one of Bahrain's most famous ancient objects. These all date to about 2100 BC. The copper statuette may have formed the handle of a mirror. Bull heads like the one at Barbar, and of the same period, have been found at Ur and elsewhere. It may well have decorated the upright of a small harp, as at Ur, and as shown in Dilmun seals.

The new homes of Hamad Town among the grave mounds.

THE BURIAL MOUNDS

The Danish excavations, and more recent work by the Bahrain Department of Antiquities, have shown that this was a major temple which continued in use for 500 years and was finally abandoned around 1700 BC. It recalls some of the most ancient temples of Mesopotamia, the temples of Ur, Al Ubaid and Khafajah.

In more recent years other ancient temples have been found in Bahrain, though none as grand as that of Barbar. Near the well of Umm as Sejour, just along the north coast from Barbar, a small temple was excavated in the 1980s, while another temple was found at Sar when the causeway was built.

The temple, town and tombs of ancient Sar date from the late third millennium BC. They have been extensively excavated in the 1990s by British archaeologists. The temple stands at the top of a rise and has two altars with crescent-shaped decoration.

The little town beside it was well-planned, with terraces of houses lining the main street leading up to the temple, and smaller side streets to the right and left. Many of the houses were designed to the same plan with a square room and an L-shaped courtyard or outer room around it. Just inside each courtyard was found a low platform for holding a water jar, and a basin for washing, with even a plastered splash-back against the wall. The same arrangement has continued for 4,000 years until modern times. Remains of bones and shells found there show the inhabitants led a similar life to that of pre-oil times, keeping goats, sheep and cattle, cultivating dates, fishing, and even collecting pearls.

Looking due south from the sandy crossroads outside the ancient temple of Sar it is possible to see the village of Aali and its extraordinary grave mounds. Twenty or more of these immense mounds, some of them 12 metres high, survive in and around the village. All were robbed long ago but their size and construction

Above: Bull's head cast in copper, found at Barbar.
Top: Altar and anchor stones at the Barbar Temple.

show a wealthy and sophisticated people living in the High Dilmun era, round about c. 2000 BC. A few finds have survived, including pottery, jewellery and carved ivory. A little female ivory figure (20 cm long), although much damaged, is a masterpiece of elegance and naturalism.

In comparison with the huge extent of the grave mounds, archaeologists have long been puzzled by the few signs of living habitation in ancient Bahrain. Sar has provided one answer. Qal'at al Bahrain, or Bahrain fort, provides another. Discovered by the Danes in 1955 this site has proved one of the most exciting and important in all the Gulf. Excavation and study have been continuous, with a French-led team at work for the past 20 years.

The site is a huge sandy mound of 10 hectares, close to the north coast, near the present Al Seef district. It is clearly visible across the palm groves to the north from the Shaikh Khalifa bin Sulman highway as it approaches the flyover across the Budaya road.

The visible fortifications were known to be a large fort built by the Portuguese in the 16th century. However it soon became clear that much else lay beneath the surface. A city was found, originating about 2150 BC and continuing in use for 3,000 years, well into the Islamic era. It had a defensive wall, a stately building, streets, houses and all the clutter of everyday life accumulated over centuries. Thus Dilmun had a capital at last (see chapter 7).

BAHRAIN SEALS

In every ancient Bahrain site, and far beyond the limits of Dilmun – as far as the Indus Valley in Pakistan and even the Mediterranean – quantities of little round stamp seals have been found. These were the seals and hallmarks of the Dilmun traders. Each was as individual as a signature.

The earliest seals were made from the cone of a shell cut across to expose the whorled pattern. Each pattern, strangely enough, is different. On the upper side, two little holes were drilled so that the seal could be suspended from a piece of string, probably round the owner's neck. Later, more elaborate patterns were cut into soft stone, called steatite, and once again, suspension holes were drilled.

The surprisingly complex scenes tell us a great deal about the lives and beliefs of the inhabitants. They show gods, men, women, boats, palms, and above all, animals usually in connection with the former. Those depicted included bulls, antelopes, gazelles, snakes, turtles, fish, ducks, birds, scorpions: sometimes naturalistic, sometimes almost abstract, but always lively.

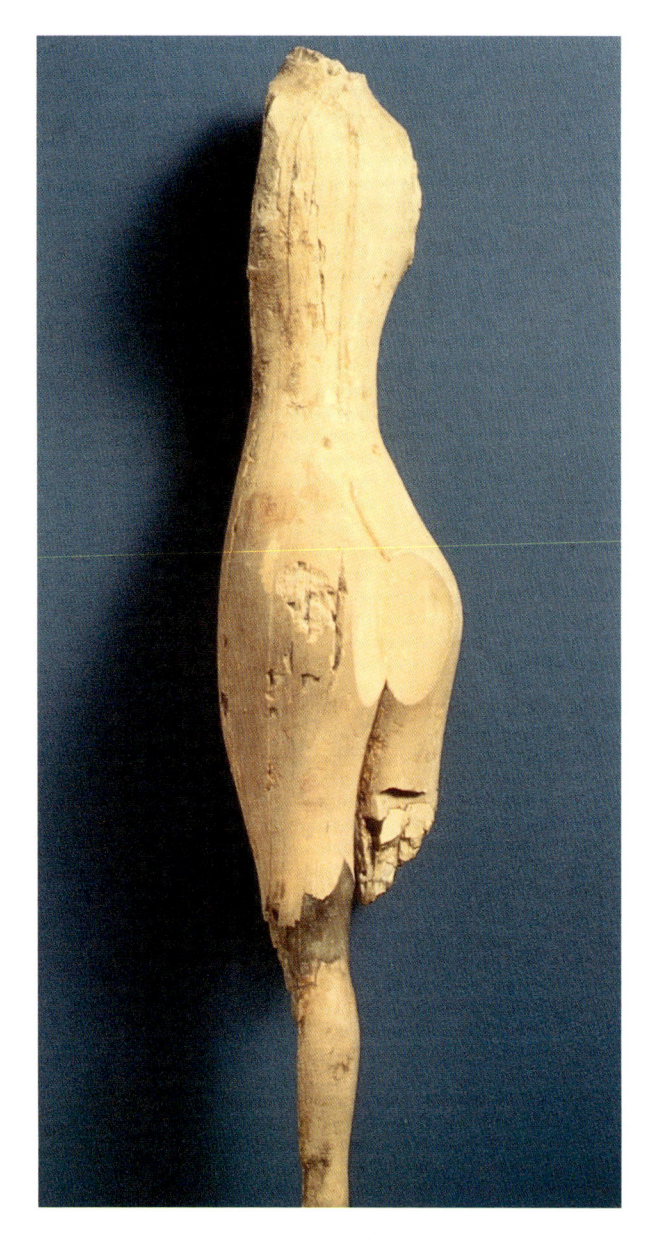

Above: A seal showing two men in a boat, c. 2000 BC.
Top: Ivory female statuette, c. 2000 BC found at Aali.

AFTER DILMUN

The name Dilmun continued to be applied to Bahrain until the sixth century BC, but the days of the great civilisation which archaeologists refer to as the Dilmun culture ended in the 18th century BC. Bahrain's prosperity then, as now, depended on the peace and prosperity of the region as a whole. The collapse of the ancient kingdoms of Iraq also brought down Bahrain's flourishing state.

Around 1750 BC Mesopotamia was invaded by the Kassite people (about whom little is known), whose influence was felt along the Gulf. There is no evidence that any of the dominant powers in Mesopotamia actually invaded Dilmun. Rather, they would continue the links of trade and political influence by appointing a governor. Around 1500-1450 BC Kassite power arrived in Bahrain. A recently discovered stele (now in the museum) from Qal'at al Bahrain has a Kassite inscription referring to a governor of Dilmun circa 1350 BC. The Kassite period at the city is reflected by some poor quality building, but also by some elegant pottery vases. Many of these tall slim pieces, of white or beige unglazed clay, were found in a remarkable series of graves – dug down into the ground at Hajjar, not far from the city.

The Kassites were succeeded by the Assyrians in Mesopotamia (1200-600 BC) and we know that King Sargon II of Assyria received gifts from Uperi, Ruler of Dilmun, in 709 BC. Two further Assyrian rulers of Dilmun are mentioned in the records: Qana in 689 BC, and Hundaru in 650 BC.

An impressive palatial building (whether palace or temple is still unknown) has been excavated at Qal'at al Bahrain. It has a handsome gateway, five metres high, of finely cut and dressed stone (see page 63, chapter 7). The evidence shows this building to belong to the fifth century BC when power on the mainland was in the hands of the Achaemenians of Persia.

The Danes made two remarkable finds which were buried under the floor of this building. One was of a series of 14 lidded bowls (dated circa seventh to fifth century BC) in which lay the skeleton of a coiled snake with a single bead at the centre. In one instance the bead was a pearl. Obviously the bowls were of ritual significance: but of what? Links have been made with the legendary Gilgamesh who, 2,000 years earlier, had been cheated of the flower of immortality (perhaps a pearl) by a snake. However, no one is really sure of the meaning of the 'snake bowls'. The other find was of some 10 earthenware 'bathtub' coffins, coated with bitumen, dated circa seventh to fifth century BC. With them were found some complete 'drinking sets' similar to others in Syria/Palestine.

Excavations of the 'city' at Qal'at al Bahrain, with the restored Portuguese fort behind.

A vase of the Kassite period, about 1500 BC.

A chlorite jar made around 4,000 years ago.

Dilmun continued its relations with Mesopotamia after the fall of the Assyrian empire (612 BC). The famous King Nebuchadnezzar of Babylon received a gift of dates and prickly pears from Dilmun for one of the New Year festivals. However, after the defeat by Alexander the Great of the Achaemenid empire (first led by Cyrus the Great of Persia who conquered Babylon in 539 BC), the old world of Mesopotamia disintegrated.

The next phase of Bahrain's ancient past, prior to the coming of Islam, has been named the 'Tylos' period. This is because Greek and Roman historians referred to the islands as 'Tylos', perhaps a corruption of 'Tilmun'. After the death of Alexander the Great in 323 BC, Eastern Arabia and the Gulf came under the successive influence of the Seleucids, the Parthians, and the Sassanians, all of whom were naturally desirous of keeping up trade links via the Gulf. Many finds of pottery and jewellery from the Tylos period have been made, at the city at Qal'at al Bahrain and a series of large graves along the north coast. Incense burners have also been found, which show the importance of a new trade route that had grown up linking south Arabia to the Mediterranean world. The incense caravans went by a western and an eastern route through Arabia. Bahrain was a link in the eastern chain. Pearl fishing is also increasingly mentioned in this period, providing more luxury for the Roman world. Cleopatra dissolved her pearls in wine and drank it to entertain her Roman lover, Antony. Perhaps they were Tylos pearls.

BAHRAIN MUSEUM

In 1988 a worthy home was opened for the display of the rich collection of ancient objects unearthed to date in the islands. The Bahrain National Museum, which houses this unique collection, has been beautifully designed to show the objects to their best advantage and to provide extensive information about them. The museum crowns the achievements of Shaikha Haya Al Khalifa, the first professional Bahraini archaeologist, and for many years Assistant Under Secretary for Culture and National Heritage.

One hall of the museum is arranged with reconstructions of the ancient tumuli, explaining their structure and content, and bringing these enigmatic mounds alive by means of models, photographs and plans. In another hall the objects found in the tombs, temples and city of ancient Dilmun are on display, while in a third hall are the objects from the 'Hellenistic' period of Tylos, and the succeeding Islamic period. In addition there is an ethnographic section, showing traditional life and customs, plus an interesting section on the natural history of the island. The museum cannot be too highly recommended, for anyone in the least interested in the history of Bahrain.

THE BURIAL MOUNDS

The two-storey cubic blocks of Bahrain's museum bordering the channel separating Manama and Muharraq.

The ethnography section of the Bahrain National Museum.

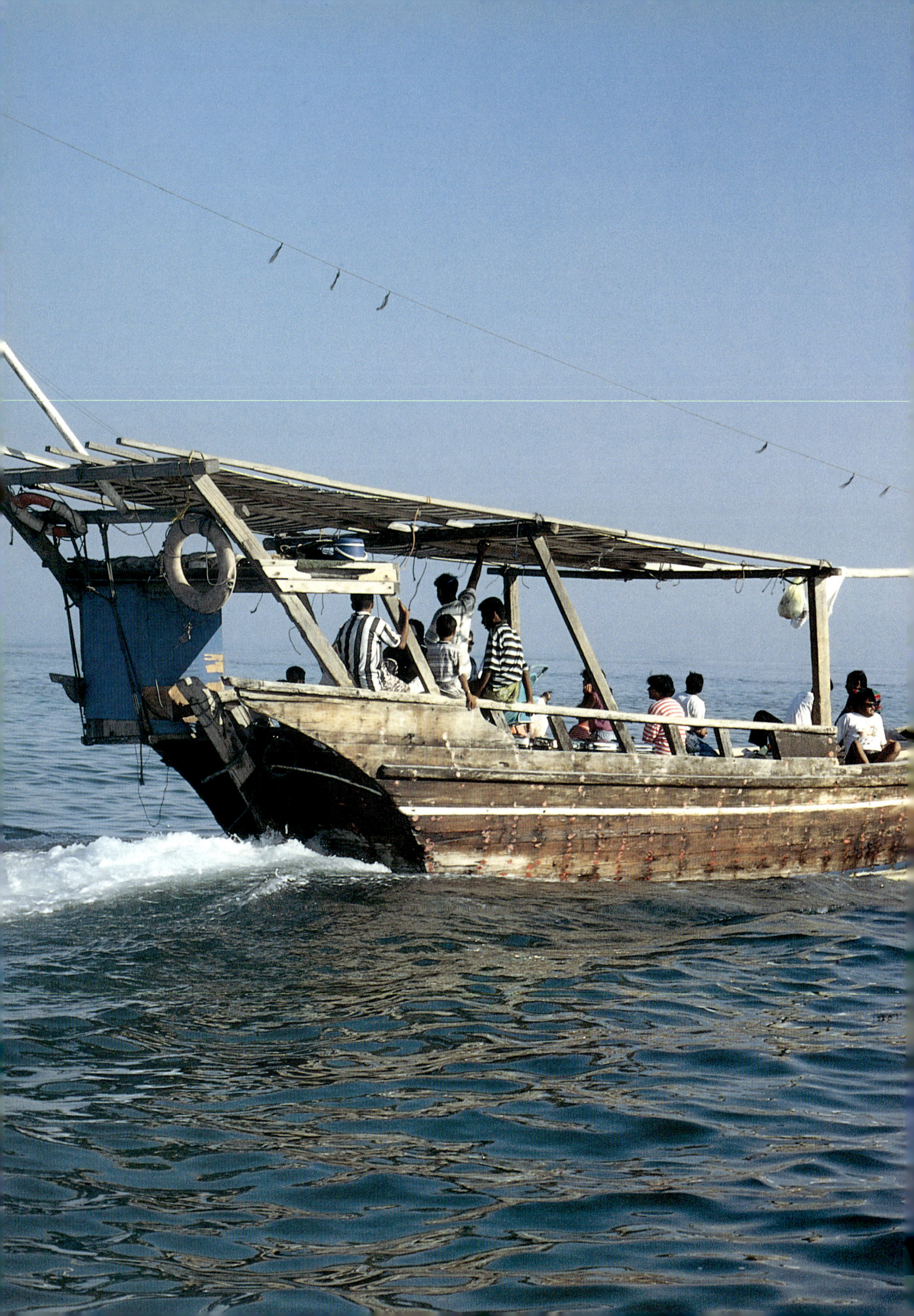

Chapter 3

A SEAFARING NATION

The people of Bahrain were seafarers from earliest recorded history, and in this area written records are more ancient than anywhere else in the world. They learnt from very early times to take advantage of their position on the great trade route between the rich civilisations of Mesopotamia and the Indus Valley (Iraq and Pakistan in today's terms) to develop a prosperous transit trade as middlemen.

Their sturdy boats plied the waters of the Gulf and the Indian Ocean beyond and sailed up the rivers to the cities which generated this trade. In the 24th century BC, King Sargon of Akkad wrote that he "made the ships from Meluhha, the ships from Magan, the ships from Dilmun tie up alongside the quay of Agade". In modern terms, Meluhha, once the Indus Valley, is now Pakistan, and Magan is Oman. For centuries, maritime trade was the lifeblood of Bahrain.

The achievement of the Bahraini merchants was all the more remarkable in that they had little to contribute, by way of local produce, to this flow of trade. They may have had a surplus of dates, for dates have been found in the ancient tumuli, and they were probably already diving for pearls, but apart from that the islands fared poorly compared with the copper of Magan or the timber, spices and semi-precious stones of Meluhha. Poorly, that is, except for their expert seamanship; but that was enough to ensure a high level of prosperity for the islands as a whole.

It would be interesting to know just what sort of boats they used for these daring voyages of long ago. So far no ancient vessel has been discovered under Bahrain's shallow seas, nor in any of her vast number of burial mounds, as has been the case with Egyptian and Viking ships. But there are a few clues, in the shape of ancient illustrations of boats, and in a tiny picture on one of Bahrain's famous stamp seals, (see page 20).

This shows a little boat very like the *huwairiyah*, the palm-frond canoe still sometimes used today to place

In the past, thousands of men set out in wooden dhows, for the pearl banks each summer.

nets near the shore or to ferry goods out to anchored fishing boats. These little craft may well have been the earliest vessels on which men ventured out on the waters. They are built entirely of local materials, all the product of the palm tree. Palm-fronds are tied together with cords and the craft is kept buoyant by filling the space below the deck with the porous stumps of palm-fronds (today replaced by polystyrene). They are good for short trips but eventually may become waterlogged.

The ancient seamen of Dilmun may have used ships resembling the *dhows* which are still very much in use around Bahrain's shores. The type certainly goes back to the era of the Portuguese, who gave it some features such as the characteristic square stern.

Arabs do not use the word *dhow* and can look puzzled when foreigners use it. They have particular names for particular types, such as *shu'ai* for the square-sterned fishing boat, *boum* for the larger sharp-sterned vessel and so on.

Dhows are still the almost universal larger fishing boats, and dozens at a time can be seen any day fishing not far out from Manama or any coast, but most of them now have fibreglass bodies. The traditional building yards are consequently in serious decline. Only a handful of boats built from teak alone are now produced each year. *Dhow* yards – for both ancient and modern types – exist in Manama (just beyond the Pearl roundabout sign to Al Burhama, on what was once the shoreline), at two yards on Muharraq, and at the Sitra Fisheries yard.

A teak boat may take up to six months to build. Its teak will have come by *dhow* from India. The techniques and tools used have changed little since ancient times. The keel is laid first, then the planks are fitted to it, and finally the ribs are placed on the inside, the opposite way round to boat building in the West.

On the water it will need a crew of five men if it is going on long journeys. For, despite its principal use for local fishing, many *dhows* still go on trading journeys, to Iran, Dubai, even India, taking foodstuffs and light cargo. There is still room for modest enterprise on the sea, among this most enterprising people, even in the age of the huge sea container ship. But the great days of adventure are over, when, after the invention of the lateen or triangular sail, *dhows* would sail as far as the China seas.

PEARLS OF BAHRAIN

Until the 1930s pearls were Bahrain's major source of wealth, and much of the island's population was involved with the pearling industry, one way or another. Each summer the fleets set out from all the coastal towns and villages, heading for the oyster banks on reefs out at sea. They would spend the four hot months of summer out

After a fishing expedition, a dhow rests in tranquil seas.

there, diving each day for pearls. And there were shorter diving trips in spring and autumn, when the waters were still just warm enough for the divers to work.

Sir Charles Belgrave gave the following description of the fleet setting out: "It was evening and the tide was full. The graceful ships, like Roman galleys, with huge lateen sails, moved smoothly through the iridescent water, silhouetted against the sunset sky. The sound of the sailors singing and the throbbing of the drums was borne across the water."

They were destined for a tough four months' work. Each boat carried its complement of divers, men who could stay under water for nearly two minutes, and dive to a depth of 20 metres. Most dives would be for half that time and depth, however, and would obtain around 10 oyster shells. The diver had a stone weight attached to his rope, and put a bone peg on his nose. When he needed to come to the surface he tugged on the rope and his partner would pull him up. He handed in his basket of shells, rested a few minutes, then dived again.

In the morning, when they were easier to prise apart after a night out of water, the shells were opened. The men placed any pearls they found between their toes, until the captain collected them. Pearl merchants came out to the fleet from the town, to select their pearls. Bahrain was the main market for pearls in the Gulf and her pearls were rated the finest. "The merchants of Hormuz come to Bahrain to buy seeds of pearls to be resold in India with enormous profit... they are called the true oriental pearls for, although pearls are to be found in many places... none of these can be compared to those of Bahrain," wrote Diego de Canto in the 16th century.

Bahrain's pearls had long been famous by the time he wrote of them. An Akkadian record of around 2000 BC mentions a "parcel of fish eyes" from Dilmun, which may signify pearls. Later come the "snake bowls" with their ritual pearl, from the city at Bahrain fort. And by Roman times Pliny was writing that Tylos was "famous for the vast number of its pearls".

By the beginning of this century pearling was still the major occupation of the country's fleet, as recorded by J G Lorimer (collecting facts on the Gulf in 1915). He noted that 100 boats were used for trading, 300 for ferrying, 600 for fishing, and 917 for pearling, out of some 2,000 boats operative around the islands.

In the 1930s, however, the value of pearls suddenly crashed through a combination of the 1929 world slump and the introduction on world markets of the Japanese cultured pearl. The people of Bahrain would have had a very hard time indeed, as did their neighbours elsewhere in the Gulf, had oil not been discovered on the island at just about the same time. Very soon the oil industry was providing employment for large numbers of Bahrainis

A dhow under construction at Muharraq.

Pearling once provided the main employment for the islanders.

Fishermen at Zellaq, west coast.

A SEAFARING NATION

A traditional teak dhow under construction.

and the pearling industry was in due course abandoned. Today some of Bahrain's merchants still have good collections of fine local pearls for sale, but few people make their living by them any more.

FISHERMEN OF BAHRAIN

The shallow seas around Bahrain teem with fish which are attracted to the old coral reefs there. So fish and dates have always been the staple diet of the coastal settlements of Bahrain. The earliest indications of human settlement on the island are mounds of discarded seashells on former shorelines, and prehistoric settlement sites reveal stone net sinkers and little fish hooks.

Today the fish section of the Central Market in Manama gives a colourful display of the many varieties of fish caught in these warm waters: *hamour* (grouper) and *chanad* (king mackerel), *saafi* (rabbit fish) and giant prawns are among the most popular but there are dozens of other species, in a brilliant array of colours, and all worth tasting. So vital is the fishing industry that where stocks have been depleted because breeding grounds were destroyed by dredging and land reclamation, the Government has created artificial reefs

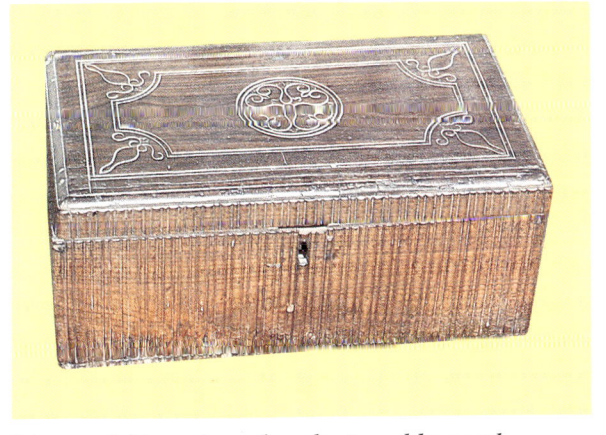

Stone weights and wooden chest used by pearl merchants.

A fisherman of the 1950s preparing bait.

Fresh fish being sold on the streets of Manama.

with old car tyres strung together and sunk offshore, to encourage further breeding.

The Government also helps the islands' fishermen by providing a mobile workshop which brings maintenance equipment for boats and motors out to the villages. Today most fishermen use fibreglass boats with outboard motors, usually carrying a pair of motors for extra power, and in order to have a reserve.

Nevertheless, traditional inshore methods of fishing are still widely used. The *hudour*, or fish traps, made of palm-frond fencing, still fringe the coastline. They look like giant arrow-heads pointing out to sea, at high tide the fish swim in past them, as the tide goes out the fish swim alongside the central fence and are guided by the side fences into the rounded 'head' of the trap where they are stranded as the water flows out behind them. The fishermen have then only to wade out to their traps to collect their catch.

When the traps needed repair, a group of men from the village would wade out and replace the broken fencing; it took a week to replace a whole trap. Today quite a few traps are made with wire mesh supported on metal pipe uprights, but made to the old design.

Another kind of trap which is becoming ever more popular is the *garageer*, first introduced in the 1950s. They are huge wire-mesh baskets with a funnel entrance

Model of a dhow for prospective customers.

into which the fish are enticed by a bait within; once in they can not swim out again. These traps are made in many of the villages, and also in Manama, beside the *dhow*-building yard.

The long streams of wires are stretched out over the ground, the maker weaves a little circular wire mat, the top of the trap, then sits on it to build up the sides around him until he seems to be working in a cage. These traps only last a few months in the corrosive sea-water so new ones are always in demand.

Perhaps the most lasting impression of Bahrain's fisheries, however, is also that on the smallest scale. All around the coasts men wade out in the shallow waters to catch the shellfish, crabs, shrimps and other small fish which come close inshore. They carry small nets of one kind or another to make the catch, which they put in their baskets. So shallow are the inshore waters that they may wade out half a kilometre or so and still have water only up to their waists.

Finally, perhaps the oldest method of them all still exerts its age-old fascination. On every quay and jetty men and boys cast their hand lines, or balance their rods, reacting with a quick flick of the wrist to the slightest tug on the line.

Such a slow way to fish it seems, yet so simple and so very satisfying.

Two men working on their beached boat.

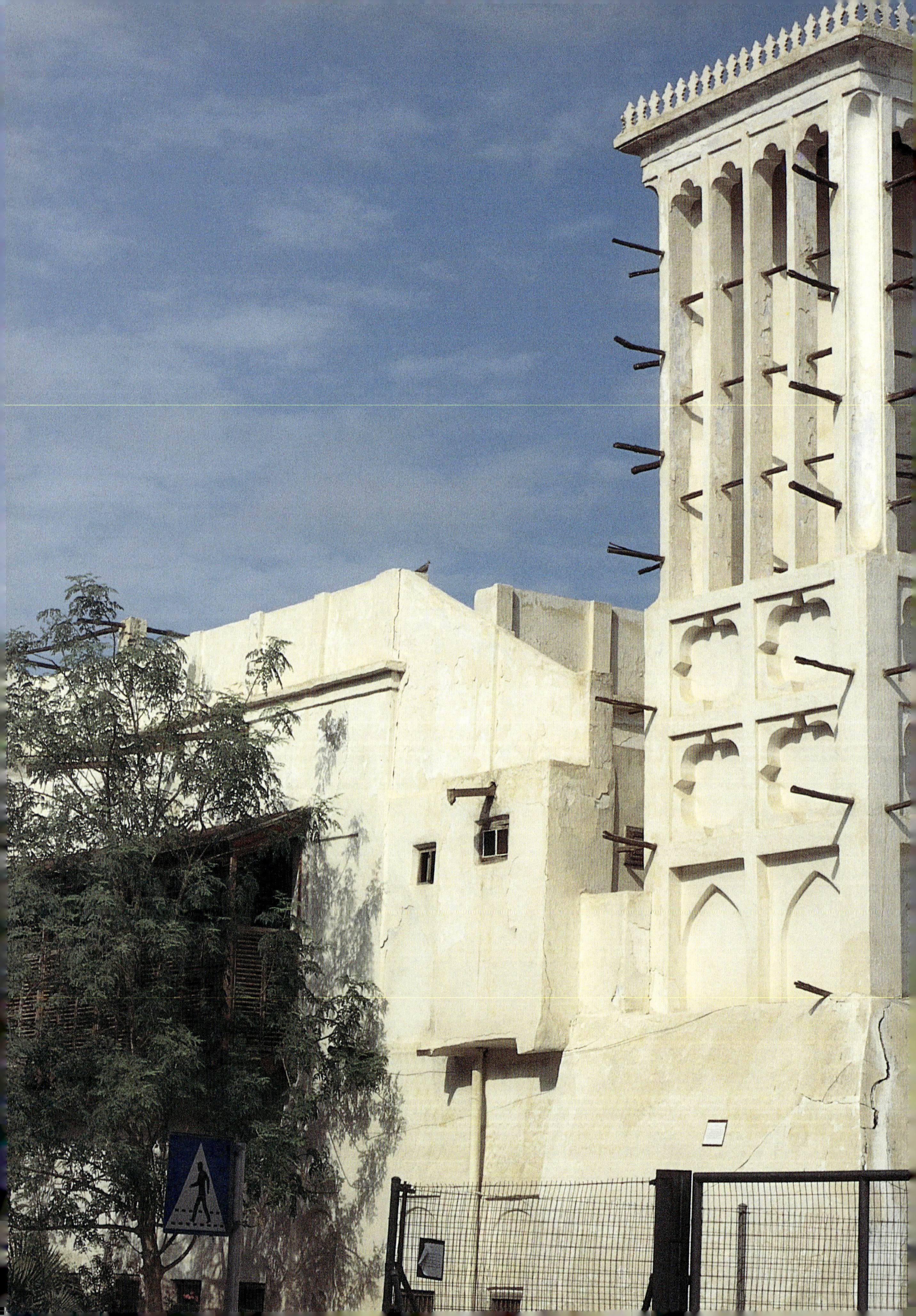

Chapter 4

A SENSE OF STYLE

Bahrain's long tradition of art and craft, stretching back 4,000 years, can still be appreciated today. Her style of architecture, whether in simple cottages, or old town mansions can still be seen, while the weaving, pottery and woodwork of the island are still alive and well today.

The traditional crafts and buildings are typical of the styles of the Gulf region, made with local materials and well-adapted to local conditions. All might have been lost, with the rapid changes in lifestyle since the discovery of oil, had not the Government encouraged craftsmen to continue their trade, and begun also to renovate some of the best of the old buildings.

VILLAGE CRAFTS

Crafts in Bahrain appear for a very long time to have been concentrated in the hands of a few villages whose people became specialists in a given calling and sold their products to others throughout the islands. To some extent this specialisation could be explained by the availability of raw materials in the neighbourhood, such as the presence of clay in the hills near Rifaa which fed the potteries at Aali for instance, but this was not always the case. Any village might have produced a surplus of palm-frond baskets, but only a few did so; any village might have specialised in weaving or embroidery, but again only a minority did so.

The villages which were centres of a flourishing craft were more prosperous and dynamic than their neighbours. Perhaps their people had always been more energetic; or did these cottage industries, handed on from one generation to the next, generate an added vitality in the families who practised them?

Fuad Khuri, who studied Bahraini society in the 1970s, recorded that the traditional craft villages – Diraz and Beni Jamra for weaving, Sitra for palm-frond baskets

Traditional house with windtower, Awadiya quarter, Manama.

This simple mosque at Ain Adhari has a traditional ceiling of mangrove poles and palm-frond matting.

Unglazed pots bake in the sun before being transformed into the traditional narghileh – hubble-bubble pipes.

and mats, Aali for pottery and lime, Busaibi and Sanabis for embroidery, and Jidd Hafs for drugs made from the flowers, pollen and buds of the palm tree – were larger and more influential than others: "The combination of craftwork and private landholding has earned them social prominence throughout history; many political leaders, men of letters, theologians and jurists, who have attained fame and reputation in Bahrain and in the world at large, came from these settlements."

Today weavers still work in the traditional way at Beni Jamra and basket-makers at Karbabad (see chapter 7); the potteries and lime kilns of Aali are as active as ever (see chapter 9); and wooden *dhows* and metal coffee pots are still made in Manama and Muharraq. The craftsmen can be visited in their workshops and products purchased on the spot. There are also a number of government-sponsored craft workshops where artisans also sell their wares. There is a large centre in a handsome building that was once a girls' school, on Isa Al Kabir avenue in Manama, and another in the west-coast village of Jasra, while the Tourist Shop in Bab Al Bahrain has a large stock of wares.

The craftsmen have remained true to tradition in their work, introducing only very slight modifications to make their products more appealing. The weavers today weave with coloured threads, replacing the uniform black *abbayas* which they made 20 or so years ago; the basket-

A young potter at work.

Ceiling of palm-frond matting and mangrove poles.

Traditional coloured glass windows help to cut the glare.

makers have adopted some green and purple dyes to enliven their platters and mats. In Aali the potters still make largely unglazed wares, bowls, jars, water pipes and, perhaps a sign of the times, have introduced a highly popular line in children's money boxes. Today, they make a little glazed pottery too, a technique which in the past they never practised, and also some painted wares.

The carved wooden doors, windows and balconies of the island's traditional houses have long been famous. In the Lahore Museum, Pakistan, intricately carved doors and balcony supports can be seen, highly prized work imported from Bahrain in the 18th century. Such work is less in demand today, but skilled carpenters still exist. Stained-glass window panels, which are such a feature of traditional houses, are still popular, and still manufactured.

BAHRAINI ARCHITECTURE

The simplest and one of the most common forms of architecture in Bahrain in the past was almost closer to a craft than a builder's art, and that was the palm-frond house or *barasti*. Today hardly any *barastis* survive on the islands, though a good one can be seen near the shores of the eastern village of Jaaw.

These houses, with arched roofs, were built of palm-fronds tied close together to make a solid fencing; they were often lined inside with palm-frond matting. In the days before air-conditioning they made a comfortable home, the palm-frond walls allowing the breezes to enter and sheltering the inhabitants from the heat. Air-conditioning, however, was incompatible with *barastis* and spelt their end.

More permanent stone houses were plentiful throughout the islands, attractive homes usually built of coral blocks. The simplest of these were the small village houses of which many can still be seen, surviving though often abandoned. They were single-storey, oblong buildings with flat roofs, usually plastered on the outside and set around a walled courtyard. The rooms of both small and large houses were long and narrow, their width the length of an average mangrove pole or palm trunk; their ceilings were made

Details of the summer palace in northern Jufair.

A SENSE OF STYLE

Heavy wooden door of traditional house in Muharraq.

Above: Fine domestic architecture, Karbabad.
Right: The Al Aali shopping mall reflects the tradition of bazaar and caravanserai.

A few fine old merchants' houses in Manama and Muharraq still survive, though more dilapidated than when they or their predecessors were seen by William Palgrave in the middle of the 19th century: "Forming distinct quarters of the town are large houses of brick and stone... they are often alike, elegant and spacious, with ogival arches, balconies, terraces, porticoes, and latticed windows; here dwell the nobler and wealthier inhabitants, and men of government."

Two notable houses, the Shaikh Isa house and the Siyadi house, close to each other on Muharraq have been restored and can be visited (see chapter 6). The Siyadi house has many decorative gypsum panels and fine painted ceilings, while the Shaikh Isa house is a splendid example of a series of buildings grouped around inner courtyards, with arches, windtower, stucco work, plaster mouldings and carved doors.

Their high-ceilinged rooms would have been furnished in the past with colourful carpets and with large cushions in embroidered white covers around the walls. A carved wooden chest or smaller wooden pearl merchant's box provided the main furnishing of the *majlis*, or sitting-room in which guests were received, of palm-frond matting above the rafters, and the roofs of compacted earth.

The houses of Bahrain were typical of Gulf architecture, designed to give as cool an interior as possible before air-conditioning arrived. They were built generally of coral blocks, an excellent material for the purpose since it was porous and gave good insulation.

Structurally they consisted of load-bearing pillars with thinner panels between. Often these panels, of thin coral slabs, were inserted in pairs, slightly offset to allow air to flow between them. The outer panel was short at the top, and the inner panel was short at the bottom, so breezes would be channelled down between them, entering the room at ground level where people would sit.

Air was also allowed in through the windows, which were glassless but closed against the heat of the day by wooden shutters, and by pierced ornate gypsum mouldings, sometimes placed above the windows. The most sophisticated air scoop of all was the windtower, a high tower built above the main room of a town house, open on four sides and at the bottom. Breezes striking the tower were guided downwards, to cool the room below; the effectiveness of the device can still be felt today, in the surviving examples.

while heavily carved large wooden bedsteads and small wooden cradles furnished the bedrooms. Such furnishings can be seen exhibited in the Heritage Centre near the Bab Al Bahrain in Manama, and in the fully renovated house in Jasra (see chapter 8) where the Ruler, Shaikh Isa, was born.

Bahrain also offers opportunities to explore unrenovated traditional houses, ranging from the small old homes visible in most of the villages, to the elegant abandoned palace west of the Al Fateh highway near the grand mosque at Jufair, southern Manama. The quiet streets of the Awadiya quarter, eastern Manama, still have windtower houses, including the exceptional Ali Reza mansion with its high portico, curving lattice balcony, high-walled garden and proud white windtower.

MODERN ARCHITECTURE

The most rapid phase of building in the islands' history has taken place since 1970. In this short space of time all the settlements have been completely transformed and enlarged, often beyond recognition.

The new buildings range from private houses and villas in the villages and suburbs to high-rise blocks in the modern diplomatic quarter of Manama. The traditional materials have been completely abandoned and today's buildings are put up in concrete and glass, designed to be cooled by air-conditioning rather than by natural means.

This vast building spurt has been a challenge to architects to design buildings in tune with their surroundings and with each other. An effort has been made, with some of the larger buildings, to produce structures with an Islamic flavour: window arches, wooden screens such as those on the Gulf International Bank building, and domes on new mosques all reflect traditional styles.

Many of the new buildings are, however, overtly modern and international in style. Glass-fronted high-rise blocks reflect the surrounding scenery, coloured tiles cover the pitched roofs of new villas, large windows let in the light with no fear today of the heat. While the first period of concrete building in Bahrain can not be rated one of the happiest, from the point of view of the islands' architecture, some of the best of today's buildings confirm that Bahrain has preserved its age-old sense of style.

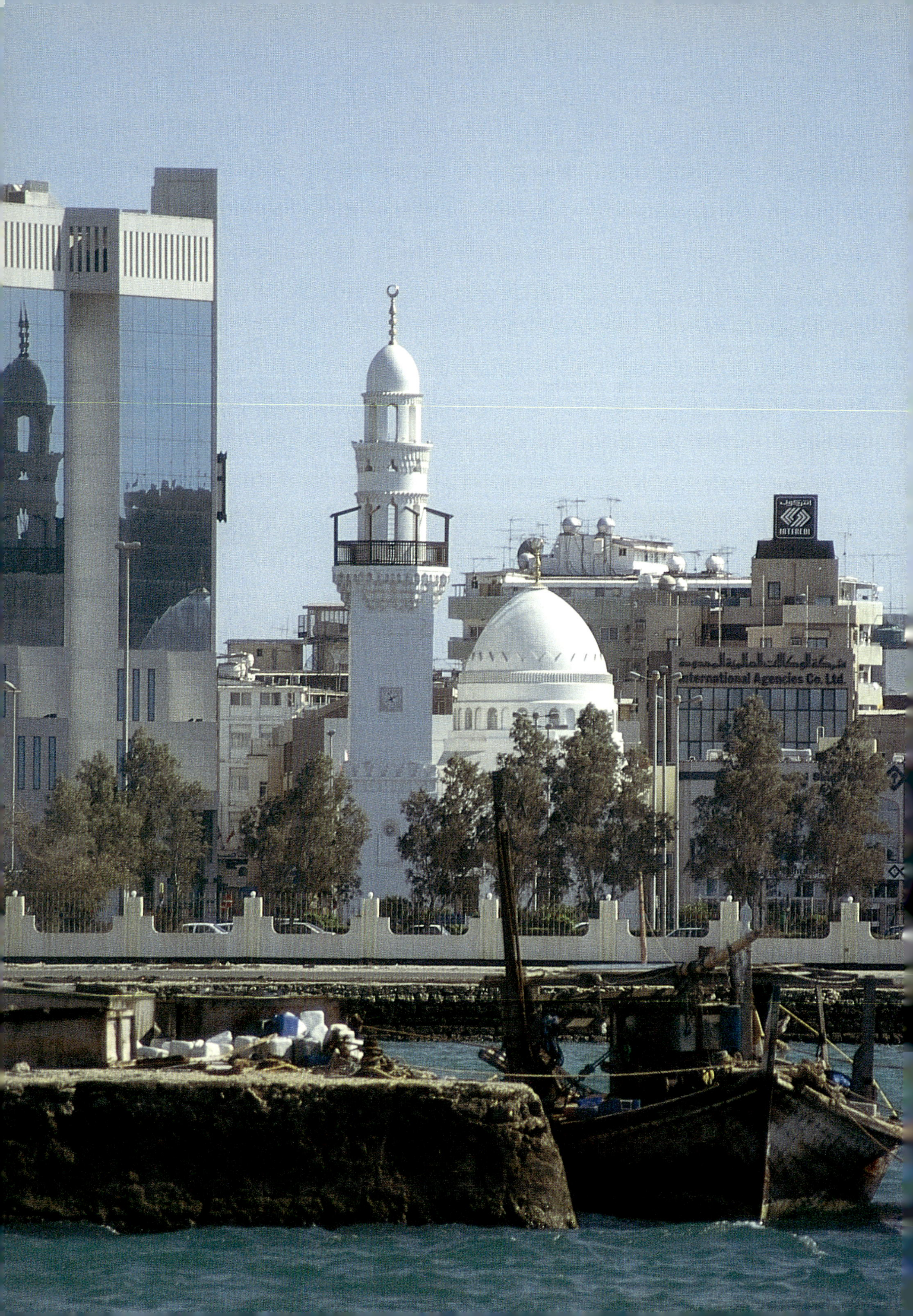
International Agencies Co. Ltd.

Chapter 5

MANAMA THE CAPITAL

Manama, the capital of Bahrain, stands on the seashore at the north-east corner of the island. The name *Manama*, which means 'the sleeping place', seems curiously inappropriate today for a modern town full of bustle and vitality.

Once, perhaps, Manama might have been classed at least as a sleepy place. In the days before cars and electricity, its elegant old houses stood along quiet sandy lanes, their living-rooms cooled by breezes funnelled in by tall, ornate windtowers. Their windows were shaded by wooden balconies, their inner courtyards sheltered by tall palm trees.

A small area of these old houses survives today, to the east of Isa Al Kabir Avenue, in Awadiya district, a little inland of the British Embassy. They appear to belong to a different world from that of the modern high-rise buildings along the seafront, two blocks away. Yet they represent the town of Manama as it was until the 1950s.

In fact, one of the chief delights of Manama, the feature which gives the town its charm and character, is the great mix of buildings of different styles and periods which stand side by side, or are tucked in among unexpected and untouched palm groves.

Unlike most towns in the Gulf, Manama did not grow in a single decade. Development came gradually over a period of 40 years or so. Old villages were incorporated as the town expanded, and they brought their palm gardens with them. Today one can still find there traces of the past, milestones of the country's history.

THE FIRST TOWN

The medieval capital of the island was known as the Bilad Al Qadim, the 'old town', although no-one knows how old that means, and in Bahrain it could be very old indeed. In the early part of this century, however, a wide

The Kanoo mosque reflected in the glass walls of the Batelco building, in the heart of Manama.

Manama's skyline reveals the capital's burgeoning development.

Windtowers provided cooling air for the house.

area of shapeless mounds still marked the site, not far from the ancient mosque of Souq Al Khamis. This town was not on the seafront and lay, indeed, part way between the north coast and the Sitra bay.

Its location was probably determined by the proximity of several of the island's best springs, the Ain Abu Zaidan, Ain Qasari and Ain Adhari. The Ain Qasari today feeds a large, shallow pool in a park; the Ain Adhari has also been incorporated into a park, approached from the Shaikh Isa bin Sulman highway.

The Ain Adhari, or 'Virgin's pool' was once some 10 metres deep: its waters were tinged blue with sulphur and it used to flow into an ancient channel about three metres broad which irrigated the great palm gardens around it. In the 1940s it was developed into a bathing place with concreted steps all round the pool and a little pavilion on one side, and a matching mosque on the other. The water rose so strongly that bathers were buffeted by the currents, almost like a Jacuzzi. Changes in the water table in recent years however have meant that Ain Adhari, like other pools, has now become virtually dry.

The Al Khamis mosque, on the Shaikh Sulman highway, is Manama's major ancient monument. The well-known silhouettes of the mosque's twin minarets rise high above its ruined walls and arches, themselves standing on a notable old mound.

The mosque was built in the early centuries of Islam – in the days of the Caliph Umar bin Abdul Aziz, it is

The ancient Al Khamis mosque.

Bab Al Bahrain, gateway to Bahrain.

A door in Manama, painted in traditional Arab blue.

said – in the early eighth century AD. There was a major rebuilding in the 12th century; an inscription over the door of the west minaret records that it was erected at that time, in "the days of the just King Abu Sinan Muhammad bin Al Fadhil bin Abdullah". The second minaret was added two or three centuries later, perhaps during major works in the 15th century.

A number of Islamic inscriptions of different periods have been found in the mosque. An inscription on a Qibla stone says it is the "mihrab of the tribe of Al Mu'alla", while there are many later inscriptions on large gravestones lying just outside the mosque. Many of these have now been collected up and taken to the Museum and the mosque has been renovated.

SOUQ AND OLD SEASHORE

In the 15th century the city moved from Bilad Al Qadim to Manama whose vital heart was, and still is the *souq* area, just inland from Bab Al Bahrain, with the addition now of the banking and diplomatic quarter nearby.

The *souq* has retained its atmosphere in spite of many modern shops with the latest goods. Its narrow lanes are full of merchants and merchandise and everyone jostling elbow to elbow. Some buildings are brand new, like the plate-glassed, marble-floored gold *souq*. But there are still plenty of intriguing alleys and lanes with bewildering displays of goods. Each lane harbours shops of a certain speciality: brightly coloured materials, gold and jewellery, spices, sandals, plastic bowls and buckets, metal pots and pans, money-changers and perfume shops; all have their corner. And all are alive with shoppers especially during the cooler hours of the day.

Another approach to the *souq* area would be to drive as far east as possible along the Budaya highway. You would eventually reach a wide open space encircling a handsome old mosque in the middle. A piazza like this is unexpected in the close-packed area: the houses and shops around it are often balconied and shuttered in the traditional way. The mosque is known as the Al Mehza mosque, named after a celebrated character, Qassim Al Mehza who was a famous *qazi*, or judge. He died in Manama aged nearly 100 years, in the 1940s. A tangle of lanes beyond this square will show you some of the surviving old houses with their sometimes exquisite wooden carved balcony and lattice work, and you will eventually emerge into a recognisable thoroughfare such as Shaikh Abdullah Avenue or Isa Al Kabir Avenue. In the latter, you may be facing the famous American Mission Hospital which opened in 1902.

The imposing archway of the Bab Al Bahrain (Bahrain Gate) was designed in 1945 by the Ruler's

Shopping near the Al Mehza mosque.

adviser, Sir Charles Belgrave, to house government offices, and provide a suitable entrance to the *souq* from the *dhow* harbour just in front of it.

At that time the seashore followed the line of Government Avenue, and the *dhow* pier was where the car parks now are. Belgrave looked out on a very different scene in those days, "a fascinating, lively, noisy place... often there were as many as 100 *dhows* anchored off the pier and tied up alongside". Today a more subdued *dhow* harbour has retreated 300 metres to the north, to the other side of the car parks and corniche highway.

The buildings along the line of Government Avenue and immediately inland of it give a fascinating picture of Manama's growth over the past half-century. The Heritage Centre, situated in the fine Old Law Courts built in 1937, houses a permanent exhibition of the domestic furnishing of a traditional Bahraini house. It also has an interesting collection of old photographs and pearl-divers' equipment. Close beside the Law Court used to stand the first petrol-filling station on Bahrain.

East of the Heritage Centre stand two rather old-fashioned blocks, the Almoayed buildings. These were considered the very latest thing in modern development when they were first put up by Yousuf Almoayed in 1956, for they were the first high-rise buildings that Bahrain had seen. A little further east stand two of today's most elegant and up-to-date buildings, the semi-glass-fronted blocks of leading banks.

Beyond the roundabout at the end of this stretch of road are the white buildings of the British Embassy. They too appear to have survived from another world, but in fact were built only in 1955, replacing one first built in 1900. At that time the sea lashed the windows in high storms, and former slaves danced once a year in celebration of their freedom on the beach at the end of the garden. Today huge tower buildings separate the Embassy from the sea, now nearly half a kilometre away and still retreating. Government ministries, foreign embassies, international banks and elegant hotels such as the Sheraton with its luxurious and popular shopping complex occupy this north-east corner.

Parallel to Government Avenue, behind the Heritage Centre, runs Al Khalifa Avenue, itself once on the seashore. Here rises the unique mosaic minaret of the Al Fadhil mosque, built by the Ruler in 1938 with the island's first oil revenues.

Nearby is the modern glass-fronted Yateem shopping centre with three palm trees preserved beside it. Husain Yateem is attached to those trees; as a boy he used to sit beneath them fishing.

Qudaibiyah palace is now surrounded by lush greenery.

The giant wheel of the fun-fair at Adhari National Park is a great attraction for young and old alike.

HOMES AND GARDENS

While palm trees in the *souq* are quite a rarity, happily they are still plentiful in the rest of Manama. As the town gradually spread inland from the seashore, the existing palm groves were incorporated into the gardens of the new villas that sprang up. In a few, though increasingly rare cases, whole palm gardens have been preserved intact. Long may these green breathing spaces escape the developer's bulldozers, for they give Manama an appeal all of its own.

Typical of the stately older buildings among the palm groves is the large Sulmaniya Hospital, on the road of that name. Its front wing still retains the pre-airconditioning style of open-fronted verandahs and loggias on ground and first-floor levels. This hospital has expanded greatly since it was first opened half a century ago.

At the eastern end of the Sulmaniya Road stands the old palace, a favourite of the Amir's grandfather. This handsome building, with its monumental staircase and ornamental gardens, originally stood not among the palm groves but outside the town. Similarly the nearby Qudaibiyah palace is shown in old photographs taken at the accession of Shaikh Isa in 1961, to be standing all alone near the sea, with no building or tree in sight.

The Qudaibiyah palace was built as a guest palace, receiving first King Abdul Aziz of Saudi Arabia in 1939. It continues to receive state visitors who bring a large entourage with them. Outside this palace and the old

Coffee and chat in the Yateem Centre.

palace a dazzling display of municipal gardening can be admired: the standard is extremely high!

Gardens and gardening are very much to the fore in Bahrain. Manama has beautifully tended public gardens, such as the Andalus and Al Sulmaniya gardens, as well as the Qassari and Adhari gardens. Roundabouts and avenues are thick with greenery and clipped trees, while promenade stretches are appearing along the new corniches created by land reclamation. One such runs north from the Al Fateh mosque, taking in the Marina Club. This is a popular club with a snug harbour for sailing and pleasure boats, as well as a beach and fitness facilities. Another corniche promenade runs along the northern shore, past Mina Manama, almost as far as the Pearl roundabout. At that point, a massive new acreage is pushing seawards. The wide level plain it has created is ideal for Friday cricket for the many Indian and Pakistani devotees, who also play on any other available empty level pitches, for instance in south Sitra.

The Shaikh Isa bin Salman highway runs westwards along the north of Tubli bay (Khawr Al Kabb) – where flamingoes wade at low tide along the muddy shore – and soon crosses below the Adhari National Park. This park, which includes the Ain Adhari, has been designed with children in mind, and is full of delightful amusements including a train, a giant fun-fair wheel and a lake with a stationary ship on it.

If you are an adult however, it is worth pausing just before you reach the actual park, to pay a visit to the

Fruit sellers in old Manama.

The Bahrain Tower and Al Fadhil mosque.

municipal nurseries which are on the right of the road leading to the park. These nurseries have the major task of rearing and supplying the thousands of annuals and other plants that so cheerfully line the city's streets. They also undertake serious experimental projects as does the Budaya Agricultural Research Station. They are engaged in an attempt to reintroduce mangrove trees, which once grew so thickly along the east coast that it was hard to make a landing.

Bahraini garden owners take horticulture very seriously. An annual Garden Show takes place each March and the prizes are awarded by the Ruler. It is the Chelsea Flower Show of the Gulf.

Modern Manama

The north-east corner of the town, the diplomatic quarter, is, as already mentioned, the showcase of the newest and most sophisticated development.

This is the district of the major banks, hotels and government offices. In this area, more than any other, one is aware of the extent of offshore banking developments in Bahrain since the 1970s. At the heyday of the boom in the region's economy, from the mid-1970s to early 1980s, more than 100 banks and financial institutions opened their doors in Bahrain.

Many of the district's buildings favour the glass-fronted style of international modern architecture. Their blue-grey glass walls reflect with surprising clarity the buildings and scenes around them. Other buildings, however, have been given a more traditionally Islamic character, their high-rise façades lightened with numerous small arches and screens.

A notable, and clever, combination of the two traditions is the Batelco (Bahrain Telephone Company) building whose pearly-blue glass façade is set at a slight angle to reflect the dazzling white minaret of the new Kanoo mosque. The two buildings, one so contemporary, the other so modest and traditional, seem symbolically linked arm in arm. They stand between Government and Al Khalifa avenues, looking over the central car park to the sea.

Modern sculpture has also found a place in this new area near the shore. In gardens and roundabouts all along the corniche road is a series of fine, monumental sculptures, reflecting various aspects of Bahrain's traditional life and connected, for the most part, with the sea. The concept of the pearl plays a central role in several of these sculptures.

With business, administration and tourism adequately accommodated in the main sector of the diplomatic quarter, more recent developments to the eastern end of this district have been devoted to culture and religion.

The pearl monument at the western end of Manama's corniche road.

The mosaic minaret of Al Fadhil mosque reflected in the glass of a neighbouring office tower.

The Grand, or Al Fateh, mosque, built in the Cairo style, eastern Manama.

One of the most prestigious of these buildings is the fine National Museum at the entrance to the causeway.

This large building, beside the sea, was opened in 1988. It is arranged in a series of two-storey cubic blocks, joined at the corners. This original design gives immense scope for the interesting display of its exhibits which can thus be logically separated into different subjects and periods.

The museum houses an extraordinarily rich archaeological collection (see chapter 2) in two of the blocks, and interesting exhibitions of local crafts, costumes and customs in a third. There is also an extensive collection of illuminated manuscripts and of historical documents, while a fourth separate, cubic building provides special exhibition halls. Additional lower buildings house classrooms, library, offices, and a shop.

Part of the appeal of the museum is the grandeur of its site. With the sea as a backdrop behind, the forecourt has been devised as a shaded atrium with a modern cloister effect created by high concrete pillars and trellises.

A little inland of the museum, and opposite the entrance to the Diplomat Hotel, is another superb exhibition hall, the purpose-built Beit Al Quran. This elegantly designed beige-coloured concrete building has a broad band of inscriptions running around the upper register. Beit Al Quran was founded by Dr Abdul Latif Jasim Kanoo in 1990. He has brought together a rare collection of manuscripts of the Holy Quran, of Islamic inscriptions, and of all sorts of Islamic written works. There is also a collection of beautiful objects – glass, pottery, metalwork, miniature paintings, textiles. From time to time carefully researched exhibitions are held. Both Beit Al Quran and the National Museum are enthusiastically visited by parties of school children who are always to be found dashing about or solemnly poring over the exhibits under the eye of their teachers. The Beit has a top floor of study and lecture rooms. It also has a mosque, in the Moroccan style.

New mosques are continually being built in Manama and elsewhere, by organisations such as the Muslim Education Society.

The most up-to-date and original of Manama mosques, however, from the construction point of view is the Al Fateh Islamic Centre Grand Mosque, on the corniche road near the Gulf Hotel. Its dome, the largest of any mosque in Bahrain, weighs 60 tonnes and is made of fibreglass. Yet the colour and texture of the fibreglass dome exactly match the artificial stonework of the rest of the building which has been built in the Cairo style.

The Beit Al Quran houses a magnificent collection of Islamic inscriptions.

The Sail monument, near the National Museum.

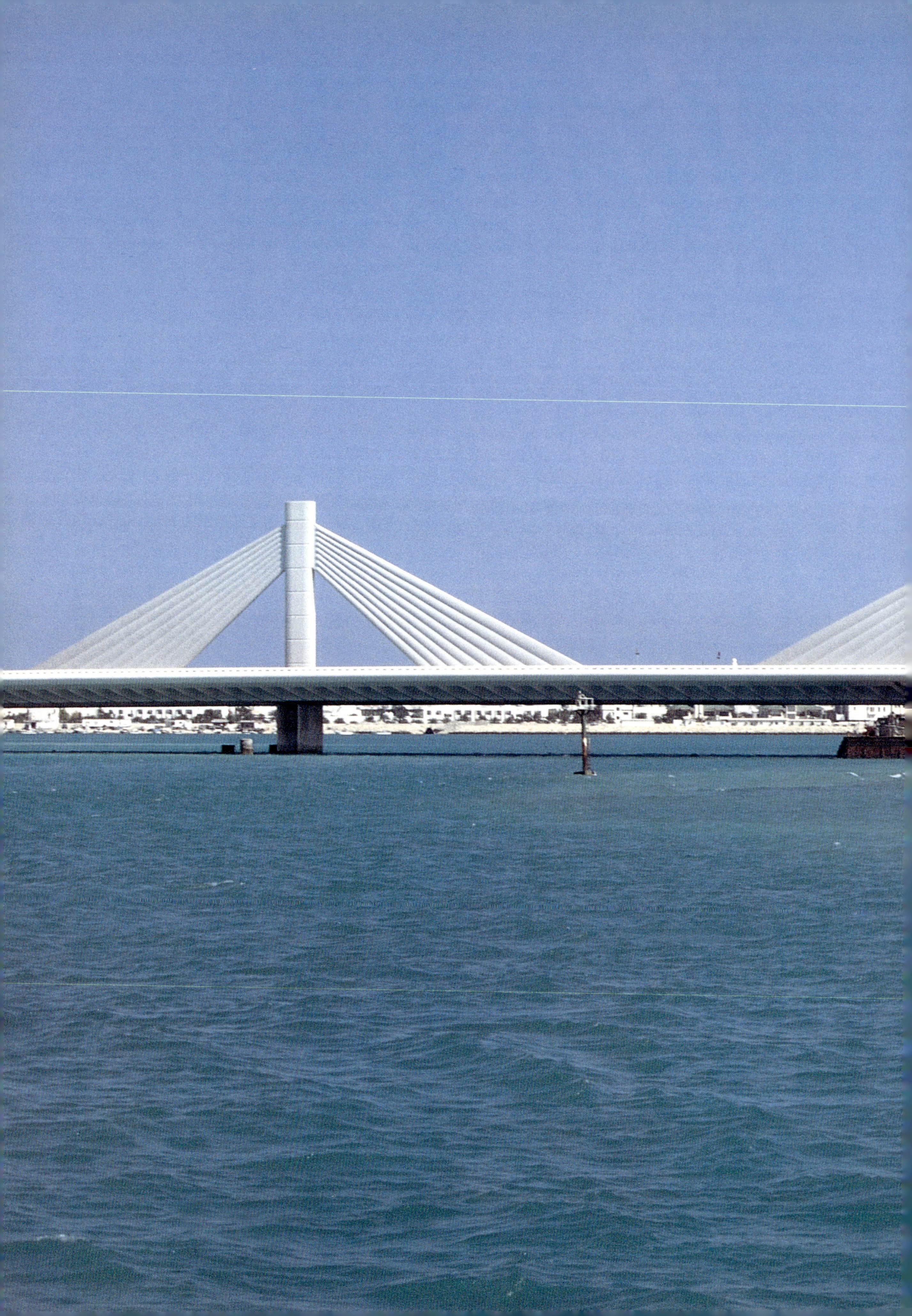

Chapter 6

MUHARRAQ ISLAND

The island of Muharraq is the first sight which most visitors catch of Bahrain, as they touch down at its international airport. Even before their plane lands, Muharraq is impressive as an atoll in a blue-green sea.

The voyager, looking down from above, observes a small A-shaped island, some five kilometres across, set in shallow, turquoise waters. All around the island giant arrow-heads, sited on this turquoise shelf, point out towards the dark blue of the deeper sea beyond. Their purpose, however, is peaceful; the island is not bristling in self-defence but simply involved in the everyday exploitation of its waters' rich fisheries. For these are the *hudoor*, or palm-frond fish traps, at their most visible from the sky above.

The airport runway extends right across the northern part of the island. It appears at first sight almost to be floating in the water, since even to the south, on the inland side opposite the terminal building, one looks across the road to water. This is in fact a large lagoon, the Dawhat al Muharraq, which penetrates to the heart of the island and was once its sheltered anchorage.

The impressions which crowd in on the visitor arriving at the airport encapsulate, within the first few minutes, so much that is typical of Bahrain: a quick and efficient passage through the airport formalities, a smooth dual-carriage highway from the door, the intermingling of land and shallow sea, and a spectacular old fort across the water guarding the entrance to the lagoon.

The dual-carriage highway was one of the first to be built in Bahrain, back in the 1960s. It runs alongside the modern houses of the sizeable town of Muharraq, with an occasional traditional old house still visible among them, then out on to the causeway linking Bahrain's two main islands. This kilometre-long causeway between Muharraq and Manama was one of Bahrain's first modern developments. Completed in 1942, it was to be the forerunner of the numerous and more spectacular causeways of the 1970s and 1980s. But this old causeway

The Sheikh Isa Al Khalifa causeway opened in 1997.

53

Minaret of Siyadi mosque.

The high-ceilinged majlis of the Siyadi house, with painted ceiling, stucco panels decorating the walls, stained-glass semi-circular windows, and shuttered main windows.

was the most vital one, connecting as it did Bahrain's two main islands and two major towns. A second causeway between the islands was opened in 1997.

MUHARRAQ TOWN

Although Muharraq town has grown impressively over the past two decades, it has retained more of the atmosphere of a traditional Gulf town than any other part of the islands. In the past it was the capital of Bahrain, a walled town inhabited by many members of the Al Khalifa family.

At the heart of Muharraq today are still the old winding lanes, small shops of an extensive *souq*, and impressive houses of the ruling family and leading merchants. The best of these houses were built in the late 19th and early 20th centuries. Two of them have been extensively renovated and may be visited: Shaikh Isa's house and the Siyadi house. The former stands on Shaikh Abdullah Avenue, the other a few minutes' walk to the north of it.

The Shaikh Isa house was built in about 1830 by Shaikh Hasan, grandson of Shaikh Ahmad the Conqueror, but was inhabited for many years by Shaikh Isa, who ruled from 1869 to 1925, and died there in 1932, aged 84. It is a rambling house whose two-storey white buildings are set around four courtyards, two of them square but the others at a slant to fit in with neighbouring lane patterns. Each courtyard has its own well.

This house is distinguished by its use of arches and columns, and above all by the fine stucco work which adorns several of the doorways. Friezes of sculpted plaster screens shade openings and windows.

It is an excellent place to explore most of the architectural features of traditional Bahraini buildings – windtowers, carved wooden doors and shutters, semi-circular stained-glass windows, mangrove-pole and palm-frond ceilings, a ridged date store for the production of date honey, and the upstairs living and reception rooms on the first floor. The house was actually inhabited until 1972 and has since been painstakingly renovated by the Department of Antiquities and Museums.

The town's Friday mosque, completely rebuilt and tripled in size, looms in brilliant white above the old mansion.

Leaving the Shaikh Isa house, walk northwards, noticing on your right another fine old house with a particularly handsome door, and in two minutes you will come to Beit Siyadi, built in the early 20th century by the pearl merchant Ahmad Siyadi. In front of it stands the delightful Siyadi mosque. The modest minaret is perfectly plain, without even a little balcony at the top,

Staircase from the courtyard, Arad fort.

and the simple open courtyard of the mosque ends in a portico supported by tall wooden columns.

Unlike the low, sprawling plan of Shaikh Isa's house, Beit Siyadi is rather like a house in Yemen, a tower-house with dependencies, the main rooms being concentrated in one ochre-coloured block, far more ornate on the exterior than is usual. Inside are splendid rooms, especially the *majlis* on the first floor, with a high painted ceiling, low shuttered windows with stained-glass, semi-circular windows above, and walls decorated with rows of sculpted stucco panels. Off this *majlis* is a smaller, lower room, set around with mirrors, the 'wedding room', where bridal couples spent their first nights together. Above it is another low ceilinged, mezzanine room with pierced screens looking into the *majlis*, from which the ladies of the house could watch unseen the activities of the pearl merchants below.

Muharraq was always primarily a seaside town, home of fishermen and pearl merchants. Today the seafront to the south of the town is alive with boats plying among the small jetties which provide an adventure playground for the boys of the town, and a seat for land-based fishermen.

A little further round to the east on Arad Bay is a small *dhow*-building yard, between the dual-carriageway

Fresh bread from a traditional baker in Muharraq.

Above: An upper majlis of the Sheikh Isa house. Below: The tall block of Beit Siyadi.

and the bay, where two or three *dhows* can always be seen in the process of construction.

In the past, Muharraq obtained much of its drinking water from fresh-water springs under the shallow seas near the island. These springs are now little used but once were invaluable both to residents and to the men on the pearling banks. They tap underground aquifers which run out under the sea from the Arabian Peninsula. Their use was described in the mid-16th century by Sidi Ali, a Turkish traveller: "The sailors, provided with a leather sack, dive down into the sea and bring the fresh water from the bottom for (the governor's) use. This water is particularly pleasant and cold in spring time. Verily, Allah's power is boundless."

ARAD FORT

Historically, it was vital to defend the hidden anchorage in the middle of the island. Today it is difficult to envisage ships sailing into this Dawhat al Muharraq, since a causeway has been built across its mouth, linking the village of Arad with the town of Muharraq. But once this was an open waterway, guarded by a fort on either side.

One fort stood on the small island of Abu Mahir, to the

Above: Little bay and boats, Qaladi, north-east Muharraq. Below: Attractive in its simplicity – an old mosque at Hidd.

south of Muharraq. Land reclamation has now joined this island to the mainland and only one tower of the original fort survives. The place is now a coastguard station, but in the early part of this century it was used as a quarantine island. On the other side of the mouth of the lagoon stands the more imposing fort of Arad, recently extensively renovated by the Directorate of Tourism and Archaeology.

The name of this fort is a very ancient one (though perhaps not so ancient by Bahraini standards). In classical times the whole island was called Arad, while the main island of Bahrain was called Tylos or Tyros. Strabo wrote of it 2,000 years ago: "As one sails further, other islands are Tyros and Arados, with temples like the Phoenician ones; and those who live on the islands say that the Phoenician islands and cities of the same names were colonised by them."

It is strange that two of the Phoenicians' major island cities, Tyre on the coast of Lebanon, and Arvad on the coast of Syria, should have the same names as the Bahrain islands at that time. So perhaps it is no empty legend that Bahrain was the cradle of that brilliant Mediterranean race, the Phoenicians, who invented the world's original alphabet. Indeed, in Bahrain, civilisation was already old long before the Phoenicians would have left its shores.

Arad fort, renovated to its former glory.

The antique fort one sees today is of relatively more recent times. It was first recorded in Portuguese miniature paintings of the 16th century, where it is shown threatened by the cannons of the Portuguese. These pictures depicted a double-walled fort, but by the time renovation started only the inner fort survived. And in its eastern tower, three cannon balls were found embedded.

However, excavations soon revealed the foundations of the outer fort, 50 metres square, and also of a plastered moat, seven metres wide and a metre deep. The archaeologists were able to show that the outer wall was the original fort, built around a well in the centre, and with just one tower at its western corner. Later three more towers were added; then the inner fort was built and the outer wall was strengthened by filling in the spaces between buttresses which had given it a cellular structure. Finally the inner fort was also strengthened with an additional inner skin wall, still visible on one side of the courtyard.

The main entrance faces the sea on the south-west side of the fort, and is approached by an unusual paved path which slopes down into the moat and up again to the gate. This would, presumably, have made it difficult for attackers to rush the door with a battering ram.

AROUND THE COAST

Muharraq island, over the past few years, appears to have put out arms to embrace the little islets around its coast. Now these are permanently linked by causeways, as satellites to the mother island. So a car instead of a boat takes one to the fishing villages of Halat and Naimand Halat as Sultah, while a dual carriageway runs along a line of former sandbanks to the artificial island of the Arab Shipbuilding and Repair Yard (ASRY).

This drydock is jointly owned by a number of Arab OPEC states. It has been increasingly heavily used in recent years and has won a well-established reputation. The drydock was considerably expanded in the early 1990s.

The causeway leading to the drydock is a good place from which to see the arrow-shaped palm-frond fish traps in use, their catch collected at low tide by the fishermen of Hidd. Today these traps are sometimes made of lengths of metal pipe supporting wire-mesh fencing, a quicker material to work than the original palm-frond fencing.

Hidd, at the start of the causeway, is a long narrow little town filling the southeastern arm of the island. The width of its promontory has recently been doubled by land reclamation and today it has been extensively rebuilt with modern houses. However, a few old houses and attractive mosques still survive there, in the narrow lanes at the heart of the town.

Surrounded as it is by the sea on three sides, its inhabitants always made their living from the water. It was a prosperous place in pearling days, the fourth largest town in Bahrain. Its schools were first opened in the 1930s; today their students have the drydock and the airport as local employers, but many work much further afield as well.

The villages of the north coast, between the airport and the sea, have retained a little more of their old world atmosphere, though they too are being rapidly developed with modern houses. Along this coast in the past were a number of beautiful old summer palaces belonging to the Al Khalifa family, for the breezes there were fresher, coming from the north-west, straight off the sea.

Today, the fishing economy of the area is supplemented by modern animal husbandry developments in the shape of poultry and cattle farms. The Bahrain dairy farm, on the north coast, stands right on the seashore, its animals kept cool by the sea breeze, reinforced in summer by electric ceiling fans hanging from the roof of their barns. They are fed with fodder grown on nearby farms.

A little further along the coast, Dair, most northerly of the Muharraq villages, has retained an appealingly traditional seafront, its waters bobbing with fishing boats, while descendants of the islands' once-famous white donkeys browse contentedly under the shade of palm trees, their empty little carts parked nearby, awaiting the next catch of fish.

Above: White donkeys wait by the sea to carry the fish to market. Below: Old men of Hidd.

In the past, when donkeys were widely used for transport, Bahrain's donkeys were rated the best. They were larger than other donkeys and mostly pure white. Donkeys are still used for general transport in the country villages (you can hear them approaching by the jingle of their harness bells) as well as for their particular job of trotting across the flats at low tide for the fish catch to be heaved into their carts.

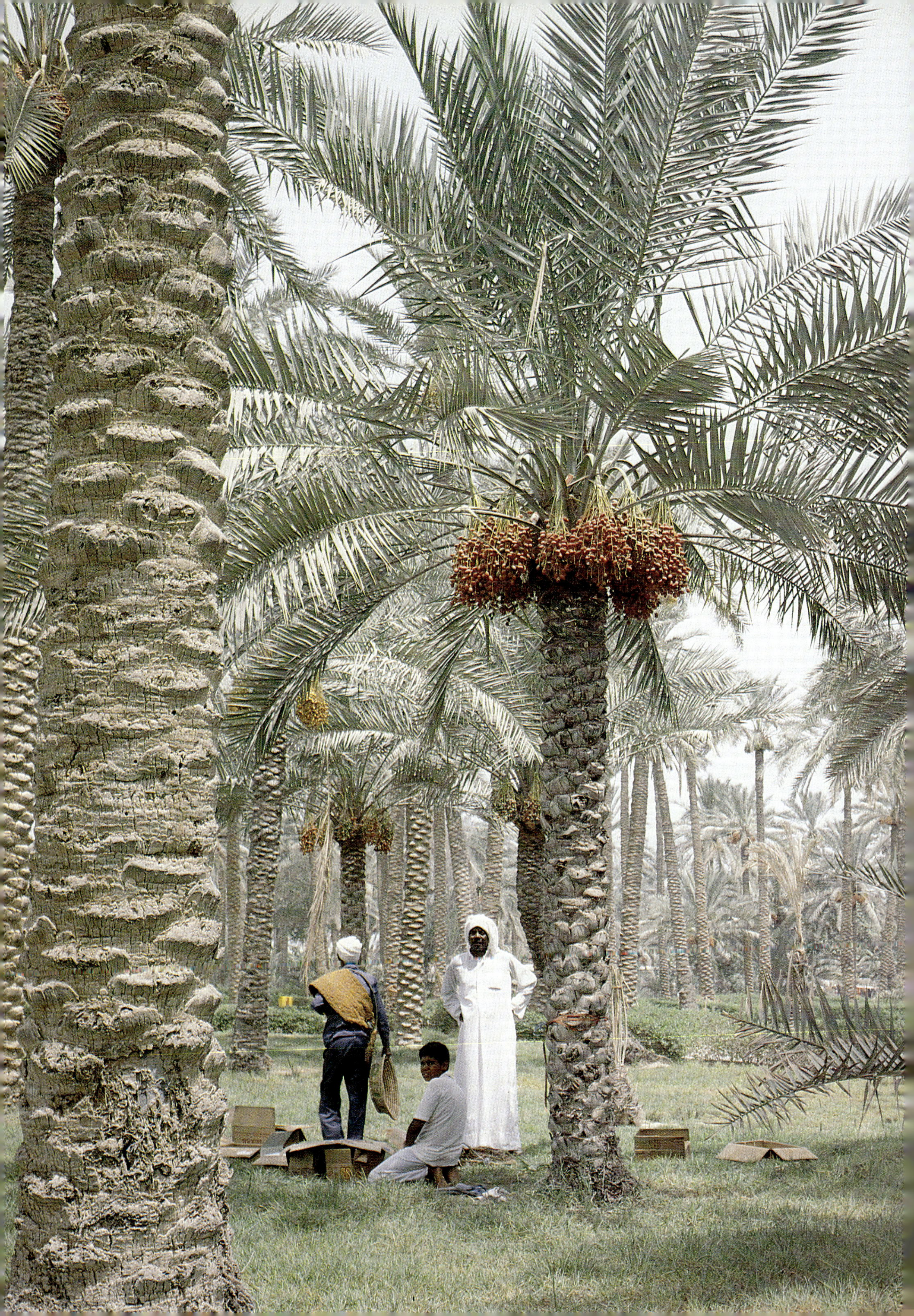

Chapter 7

THE NORTH COAST GREEN BELT

The north coast is the most fertile part of Bahrain island, with dense belts of palm groves extending many kilometres inland. Although the main road from Manama to Budaya has been built up along its whole length, and the palm trees there have much diminished, there are still wide areas of date gardens and scrub-land, especially between the road and the sea.

Bahrain's greenery has always impressed travellers. Ibn Batuta, writing in the 14th century AD, remarked: "Bahrain is a fine and considerable city, with gardens, trees and streams. Water is procured at little cost... In this place are palm enclosures, and pomegranates, lemons and cotton." The Arab navigator Ahmad Ibn Majid, writing around 1500 AD, made a similar observation: "There are a large number of date-palms of various qualities and horses, camels, cattle, sheep and goats, and flowing springs with pomegranates, figs, oranges and limes..."

Dates have been grown in Bahrain since the earliest times, and date-stones and skins have been found in ancient burial mounds. The shade and luxuriant growth must have given rise to the Sumerian legend of a land of paradise. Beneath their fronds many other plants will prosper: the fruits listed by the Arab travellers of long ago still flourish in the palm gardens, along with papayas, bananas, melons, tomatoes, alfalfa and many vegetables besides.

Date-palms demand skilled cultivation. They must be propagated by offshoots to obtain trees of the right sex, fertilised by hand in spring, and the dead fronds trimmed back in winter. Above all they require sufficient sweet water which must be provided by irrigation. When this is no longer available the fronds soon wither and die, as headless trunks around Manama show.

Among the palm groves of the north coast – dates have been grown in Bahrain since the earliest times.

61

The renovated Portuguese fort at Qal'at al Bahrain.

Until recent times Bahrain's natural springs were able to support her groves and gardens. Streams still exist (though fewer) which are full of small fish and frogs, and sometimes terrapins. White egrets can often be seen pacing up and down the ditches, and a rim of fresh green reeds will show the line of the water, often in dry, unpromising surroundings.

The most ancient sites along the north coast are centred on natural springs and it is likely that there was a cult of Enki, or Ea, the Sumerian god of 'the waters under the earth'.

First to be excavated by the Danish team of archaeologists (see chapter 2) in 1953 was the site of a once-famous well, called Umm as Sejour. Near it are the remains of a third millennium BC temple, at Diraz.

The big ring of large well-cut stones lying tumbled on a sandy ridge around a hollow can be seen today, a few hundred metres north of the Diraz temple. A fence surrounds the site but the guardian expects visitors and cheerfully welcomes them in.

The site is a very ancient one. Danish and, more recently, Japanese teams dug near the hollow and found first one, then two, narrow flights of steps leading down to a stone-built, partly-roofed chamber. This was the well-head, where the water gushed up as soon as the excavators reached it. Two headless statues of rams were found, toppled from their plinths, as was pottery of which the same type and date (third millennium BC) would later be found at the Barbar temple nearby.

The temple of Barbar is, however, Bahrain's most famous ancient temple. It stands near the village of Barbar, about one kilometre from the coast, and was identified about the same time as Umm as Sejour, from which it is only a little over a kilometre distant. This temple too was closely associated with a sacred spring. A beautifully-built, stone-lined square pool lies at the bottom of a flight of stone steps, on the western side of the temple mound.

This mound can be easily seen, to the east of the road running into the village of Barbar from the main Budaya road. A lone column stands upright, between the temple and the road.

The temple covers a low mound, consisting of the ruins of three temples built one above the other.

Excavations there have revealed fine stone walls, staircases, the sacred well chamber, circular altars and a row of large pierced stones, thought to be ancient stone anchors. Modern embankment walls reinforce the excavations, and access paths with railings allow the visitor to see the various features from close by.

The Barbar temple was first built around 2200 BC and continued in use, with enlargements and rebuildings, for about 500 years.

Four kilometres east of Barbar, and the same distance again from the western edge of present-day Manama, was a far larger mound, one which has proved among the most significant and exciting in the whole of Gulf archaeology. It is known as Qal'at al Bahrain, the 'Bahrain fort'. It was discovered and worked on by the Danes from 1955. For the past 20 years a French-led team has been at work there.

The site is a huge sandy mound, or 'tell' of 10 hectares close to the sea. To the east, the new Al Seef district, created out of reclaimed land, with the Meridien Hotel as its chief feature, is creeping up on the shoreline of Qal'at al Bahrain.

The massive Portuguese fort, built in the 16th century dominates the site and can be clearly seen from the distance of the Shaikh Khalifa bin Sulman highway as it approaches the flyover that crosses the Budaya road. This fort has recently been painstakingly repaired by the Department of Antiquities and its bastions rear impressively solid above its deep moat.

However it soon became clear to the Danes that a great deal more lay below the mound that sprawled around the European fort.

The deep excavations visible just below (south of) the fort show part of the 'city' whose residue shows it to have been inhabited for about 3,000 years, beginning perhaps

Above: The gateway to the principal building.
Below: The 'fort by the sea' (Tylos period), Qal'at al Bahrain.

in 2150 BC. A strong defensive wall was built around 2000 BC; it surrounded houses, streets, a stately building, elaborate sanitary arrangements, a date-press for making syrup, and in particular, an impressive gateway of beautifully cut and dressed stone, standing five metres high dating from the period of Assyrian power in Mesopotamia. The stately building may have been a palace. The famous snake bowls and 'bathtub' coffins (see chapter 2) were found buried beneath its floors.

The northern ramparts of the restored Portuguese fort.

Forts on the Shore

In the Tylos period, that is when BC gave way to AD, a fortress was built close to the seashore. Its outline can be clearly seen and its round towers, its entrances and courtyards can all be wandered over and guessed at, a few metres from the water's edge (see photograph on page 63). Many questions about it still remain. Strangely, nothing has been found dating from the early centuries AD to the 13th century, when coins from both Turkish dominions and China were discovered, as well as much Chinese porcelain and ceramics. That goods from China were reaching Bahrain in the 13th century was a fascinating discovery. No inscriptions have yet been found to help clarify the story of the shoreline fort.

By the 14th century it seems that there was a need to create a new defence. The fort right on the shore was given up and a fortress constructed on the site that would two centuries later be re-used by the Portuguese. Traces of this Islamic fort can be detected within the European fort.

The Portuguese began to make themselves felt in the area of the Gulf not long after their great navigator Vasco da Gama rounded the Cape of Good Hope (1498) and made possible a sea route between Europe and the East. In 1514 the King of Portugal's famous commander Alfonso da Albuquerque wrote to him about Bahrain: "Bahrain is a great power, rich in pearls, a great number of craft set forth thence to India loaded with a great number of horses and quantities of pearls." For many years the Portuguese made themselves useful to the Princes of Hormuz, a Persian clan that was semi-independent of the Shah, and who lived by their control of the all-important narrow entrance to the Gulf. Nominally on behalf of these chieftains they made several attempts upon the island, but met with set-backs such as the plague carrying off most of their forces, in 1529.

By 1560 they were in control of the island and had set about the entire rebuilding of the Islamic fort which had been built two centuries previously. Fortress building had been given a lot of attention in the Europe they had left behind and the Bahrain fort was built to the latest specifications. All the same, the Portuguese did not remain long and in 1602 they lost their fort through negligence rather than lack of arms.

Among the Villages

The names of nearly all the villages along the north coast are closely linked with archaeological discoveries. On either side of the Budaya road are dozens of burial

Farm workers under the walls of the Portuguese fort.

Date skins from a 4,000-year-old burial mound.

Huge Hellenistic burial mounds of Janussan.

The mosque at Budaya.

mounds; low sprawling, shapeless mounds for the most part, quite different from the neat, rather uniform mounds which covered the arid parts of the island.

These mounds of the northern coast each contained a number of graves and for the most part they were built about 2,000 years ago, in the times of Greek influence in the Gulf. Some of them, though, like the famous Hajjar graves now preserved by the roadside, were built long before and used over thousands of years, beginning more than 4,000 years ago.

By far the most impressive of the north coast burial mounds are those near the village of Janussan, just to the west of the road leading into the village from the main road. Here a line of huge (15 to 18 metres high) sandy mounds runs parallel to the sea, in an attractive setting with palm gardens at their foot.

Excavations of some of these mounds have revealed numerous tombs, a few of which are still visible. They date from the first century BC to the second century AD. Here, as in other graves of the same period, a glazed bowl was often placed upside down at the corner of the grave, just on or under the capstone; these bowls may have contained food or incense, for they still hold traces of ashes and organic material.

At the very bottom of the mounds different burials were found, graves of infants buried in large jars. These burials are thought to be some 500 or 600 years older than the graves in the sand mounds above.

At Shakhurah, south of the Budaya road (which artificially separates the many ancient sites), a beautifully executed Bahraini dig shows another giant mound, neatly cut down the middle. On the left or east of the road stands a sign saying 'Archaeological excavation, Directorate of Museums and Heritage'. Go beyond it and climb the 12-metre steep sandy slope behind. At the top you will not just be rewarded by a delightful view eastwards towards Al Hajjar over the palm groves, but you will be startled by the sheer cliff at your feet where archaeologists have cut down to ground level. A dozen or so graves, carefully cleaned and cleared, have been revealed. Most striking are the plastered, neat rectangular-oblong tombs (with cut-out sections at the four corners for offerings) dug about one metre into the ground, and standing 30 centimetres or so above ground as well. These tombs are of the middle 'Tylos' period, between BC and AD. Some older graves were also found.

A curious discovery was made of two sealed, intact tombs which, when opened, had no human remains inside. They contained offerings: jars, bowls, beads etc. but no body. One explanation is that these were graves made for people who had died abroad, or at sea, whose bodies could not be buried.

An open grave at Janussan, Tylos period.

THE NORTH COAST GREEN BELT

Shakhurah is also the home of the Bahrain Equestrian Association, where gymkhana events, and sometimes, informal races are held. Bahrainis and expatriates stable their horses here and can often be seen riding out along the lanes and byways of the whole area, when the heat of the day is not too intense.

Many of the villages of the area, and down the west coast too, have not only their mosque, but also a religious meeting place – *mat'am* – very often marked by an 'onion' dome of gold, or turquoise. Often too, the village will have the mausoleum of a revered religious leader. Jidd Hafs, south of Sanabis, has a particularly famous mausoleum, to Shaikh Husam bin Abdussamad of Iran who came on a mission to Bahrain and died there in 1576 AD. The little village of Halat Abd as Salih just south-west of Qal'at al Bahrain, on the road to Kerranah, boasts a walled and tended graveyard, green flag fluttering in the breeze in honour of a leader from Hamra in Iraq who died in 1044 AD. Arabian graveyards are very simple, having, as a rule, an unworked stone at the head and foot of the grave and nothing more.

In most of the villages some traditional, coral-stone houses still survive, but many are now abandoned, overtaken by modern, concrete villas. The villagers themselves have built individual new houses, while for expatriates many compounds of similar or identical villas have sprung up along the roadway.

This green, northern belt is also the site of some luxurious, private villas tucked away among the palm trees. Their owners have taken advantage of ready-made shade and greenery to develop splendid gardens beneath

Fine villa among the palm trees.

the date trees; their swimming pools are alive with the happy chatter of young children.

Many of the best gardens on the island are to be found along this coastal stretch. The lead was given early on by the Government's Experimental Farm in Budaya, first started in 1930, which introduced many new plants to the islands, and studied their care and cultivation. These gardens, sited at the entrance to the village, are well worth a visit, as is the large village of Budaya itself, a pleasant place at the extreme north-west corner of the island. It is an active fishing village, with a central district of some traditional houses, and wooden *dhow*s on the shore.

Palm gardens run along the shore, to the south of the village, and among them is one of the island's prize flower gardens. Here an extraordinary range of

Ridged trough for collecting date juice, a design unchanged up to the present day.

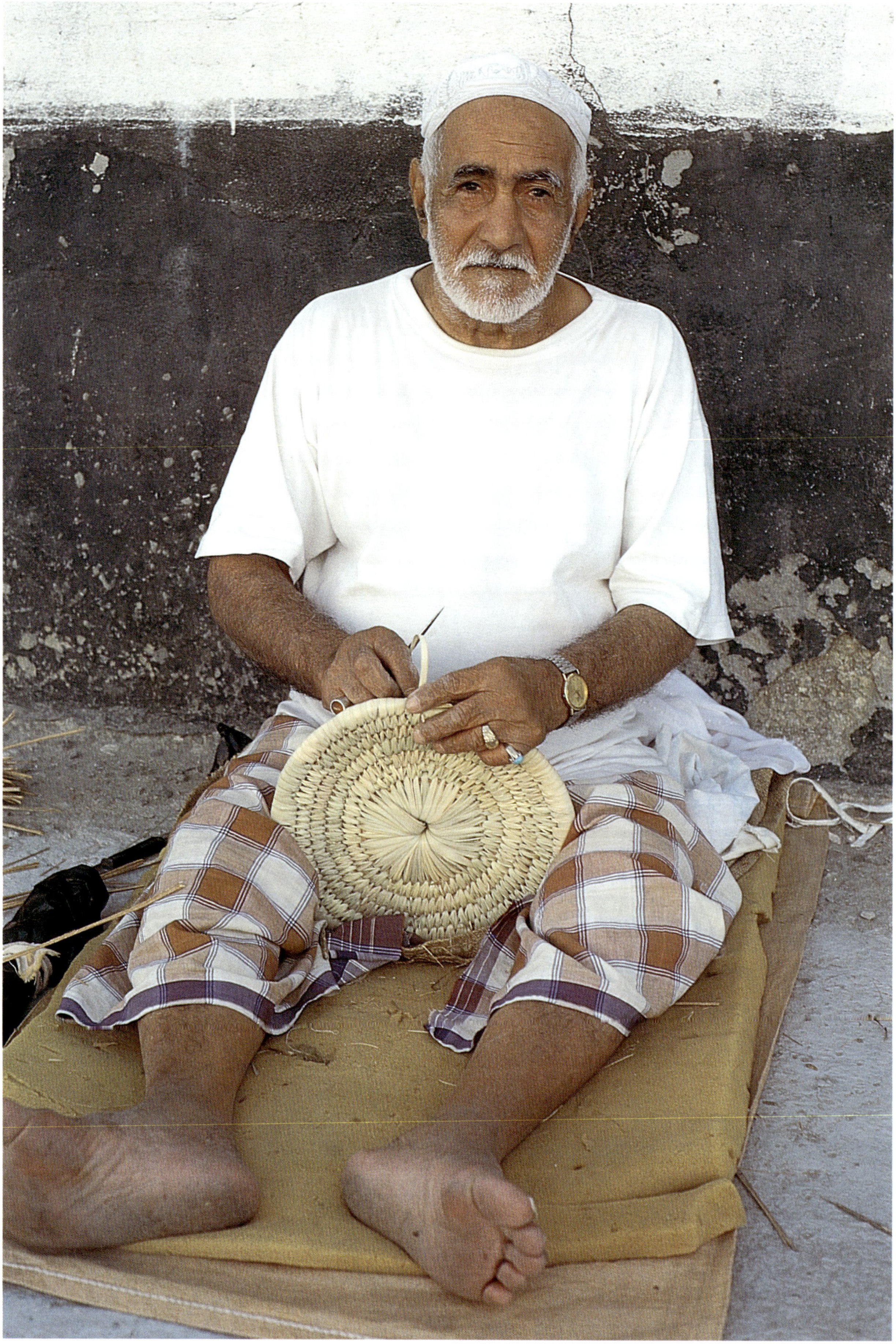

flowers – roses, sweet peas, antirrhinums, carnations, petunias, poppies and gladioli – grow in dense profusion in well-sheltered beds. Their heavy scent hangs over the gardens in the late afternoon, undisturbed by breezes from the sea only a couple of hundred metres away. Their vivid colours contrast enticingly with the sober green of the palm trees. Owners of gardens like this are often keen competitors at the Bahrain Garden Club annual show in March, which is judged by the Amir.

CRAFT WORKERS

Budaya is not the only village to have established a successful blend of the traditional and the modern. In the nearby village of Beni Jamra, just to the south of the highway before it enters Budaya, traditional ground-loom weaving is still carried on, in workshops under wood or palm-frond shelters, in the edge of the old village on the hill.

The warp threads run out along the ground for several metres in front of the shelter, under which an old man sits with his feet in a pit, the wooden loom in front of him. Rapidly he pushes the shuttle back and forth across the threads, to produce lengths of coloured cotton cloth. It takes him eight hours to weave six metres of cloth in this way.

There has been a tradition of basket makers at Karbabad, between Qal'at al Bahrain and the reclaimed land, Al Seef, where the big new shopping malls and the Meridien Hotel have been built. You will find the weavers and their work in an unmarked wooden hut, partly covered with palm-fronds, on the left (north) side of the road if you are coming from Qal'at al Bahrain. Baskets – sometimes conical with lids – mats, platters, food covers, cages to carry chickens and other birds, are all made from either the fronds or the stems of the palm leaf. Bright touches of green, purple and magenta are a recent, cheerful introduction. Further centres of this and other traditional crafts are at Jasra, and in Manama, Shaikh Isa Al Kebir avenue (see chapter 4).

Although *dhow* building is now in decline (see chapter 3) one can still see traditional teak *dhows* being made at the yard just off to the left of the Pearl roundabout (signed to Al Burhama). They are being made in ones and twos where once they were being made in dozens. The time-consuming fitting and shaping of teak has now for the most part given way to the ready-made fibreglass bodies.

Left: Weaving palm mats at Hulat Abd as Salih.
Top: Palm grove near Kerranah.
Right: Weaver of Beni Jamra.

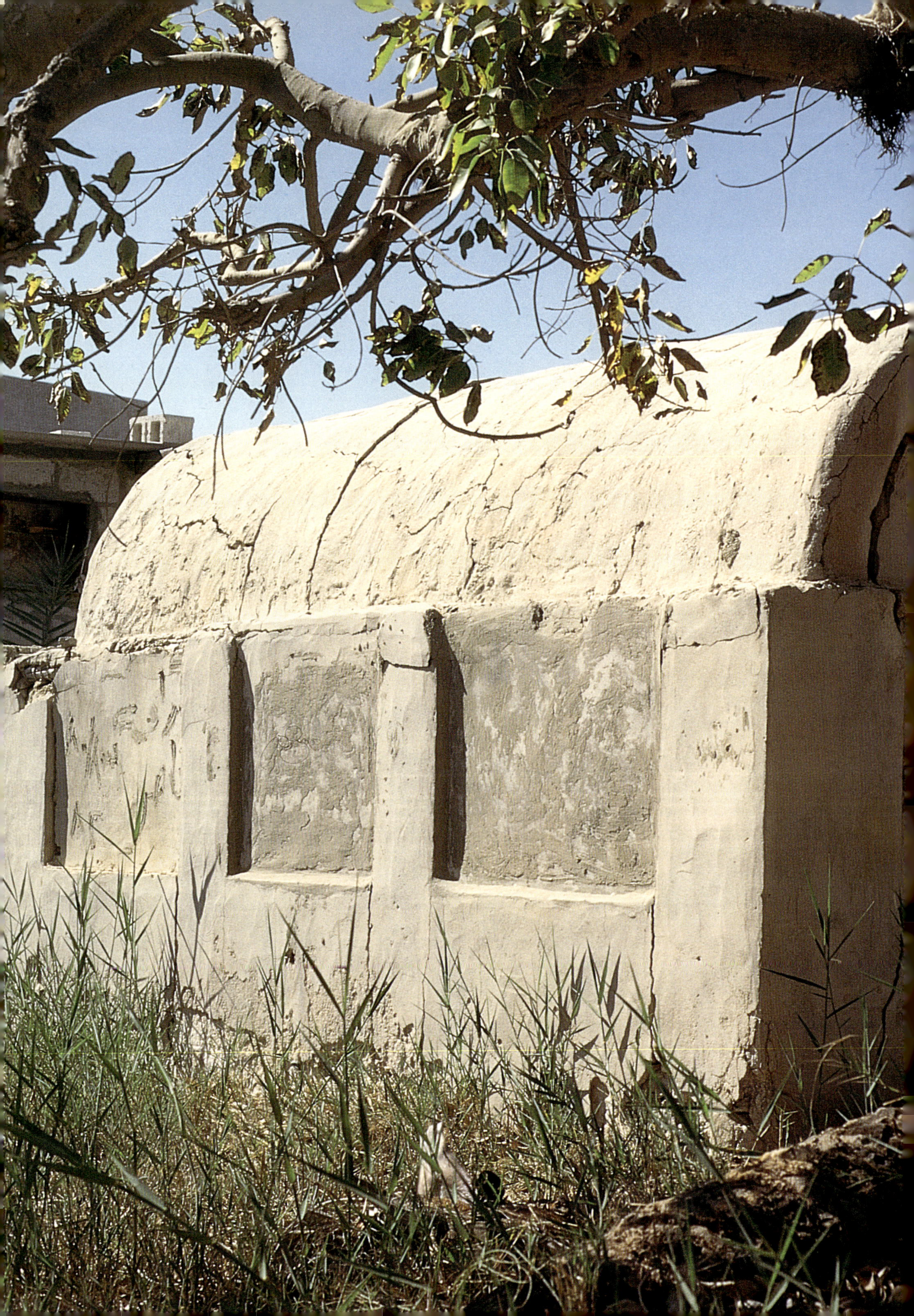

Chapter 8

THE WEST COAST

The palm groves and vegetable gardens of the north coast continue southwards along the west coast for half the length of the island. But here, along the western shores, the groves are narrower, the effort to obtain sweet water is greater.

The plantations, in fact, are hedged in by the sea on the west and by arid, rising ground to the east, the edge of the rim rock which encircles the central part of the island. This ridge was never cultivated and was, in the past, the site of the vast ancient cemeteries which covered much of the island with their strange irregular humps.

Nevertheless, it was from the foot of this rising ground that the industrious villagers of times gone by drew the water for their palm gardens. Along their shore were fewer of the copious springs which kept the north coast green. They needed to exert greater efforts and ingenuity to ensure a continuous supply of water for their crops.

They provided this by a series of *qanats*, or underground irrigation channels, running out from the rim rock to the gardens on the shore. Some of these *qanats* are still visible today, marked by a line of stone-built 'chimneys' running straight across the land. These chimneys are in fact maintenance shafts to an underground tunnel carrying water from a deep well inland, and running at a very gentle slope until it surfaces beside the palm trees. They were constructed a very long time ago using a technique developed in ancient Iran.

First the builders dug a mother well, then the first shaft, then the tunnel connecting them was burrowed out. The tunnel was supported by a pointed arch of coral rock slabs. So the work continued all along the line until the water came near the surface, since the slope of the land was greater than that of the tunnel.

At this point a 'cut and cover' technique was used: a trench was dug for the tunnel, roofed by its sloping slabs, and the earth filled in above. There are several places along the west coast where these shallower *qanat* sections can still be seen. But today they are not

Garden house, Dousari estate, Zellaq.

The causeway linking Bahrain with Saudi Arabia forms a backdrop to modern boats and old dhows.

maintained. The drop in the water table, and the ready availability of diesel pumps, have made such labour unproductive and few of them still carry water.

THE CAUSEWAY

While the *qanats* were among the major engineering feats of ancient times, the causeway linking Bahrain to Saudi Arabia is certainly the outstanding achievement of recent years. This unique, 25-kilometre-long land-link was the culmination of many years of effort, from the first feasibility studies commissioned by King Faisal of Saudi Arabia, to the opening of the completed project in 1986.

From the north-west corner of the island an immensely long bridge snakes out across the ocean, supported on pylons, for as far as the eye can see. This is the start of the causeway which leaves the island, near the village of Jasra, very close to the spot where the oil pipeline from Saudi Arabia also reaches Bahrain's shores. It runs across the sea by means of a series of bridges, artificial causeways and stepping stones on existing islands.

To drive right across the causeway requires passports and permits, and women are not allowed unless they have a male driver.

But the Bahrain section is open as far as the central island, and is well worth taking. It is an extraordinarily exhilarating feeling to bowl along this narrow strip of asphalt over the clear blue water, seeing the road rise and fall ahead, like an endless gentle switchback.

Halfway along the causeway, an artificial island

in the shape of a number eight accommodates customs and other facilities. Two high towers, one on each side of the frontier, were built to hold restaurants on the ground and top-floor levels. The view from the top is superb, and over the years has attracted many diners.

This link with the mainland has quickly proved its popularity. In the first two years of its existence seven million travellers crossed from one side to the other. The causeway runs across the northern tip of Bahrain's second-largest off-shore island, Umm Nasan. Here, sweet-water springs support extensive palm groves and there are signs on the central high ground that the island was inhabited in ancient times as well.

A little to the north of Umm Nasan are two other, much smaller islands. Jidda, the larger of the two, was the source of good building stone for many of Bahrain's ancient buildings. In one of its quarries is an inscription reading: "In the year 968 AH (1561 AD) there was completed the cutting of the 1,100th rock for mending the towers of the Bahrain fort...by the hand of the slave Muhammad bin Ahmad." In more recent times the island served as a prison too.

SAR GRAVES

Construction of the approach road to the causeway aroused a flurry of archaeological activity. The highway, as it rose over the ridge a little inland of the coast to the south of the village of Sar, cut across a dense cemetery of ancient burial mounds (see chapter 2).

Several seasons of intensive excavation revealed the

White cattle-egret waiting for some fish.

The palm gardens of Janabiya.

methods of construction of these 4,000-year-old burials, and produced a wide range of burial goods. Some of the excavations are still clearly visible on the northern side of the highway.

Here one can see the traditional burial mounds with a single grave at the centre, or occasionally an extra grave or two. But beside these mounds, which must have been for the wealthier classes, is a wide area of smaller graves, stone-built chambers each surrounded by a circular wall, but with the stone circles interconnected and almost overlapping, giving the effect of a giant honeycomb. Close beside the main cemetery was an area reserved for children.

COASTAL VILLAGES

The dual carriageway known as the Janabiya highway running south from Budaya, at the north-west corner of the island, passes between the grave mounds of Sar to the east and the dense palm groves and lush gardens of Janabiya to the west. The dilapidated *qanat* which once fed some of these plantations can still be clearly seen alongside the asphalted lane from Janabiya to Sar.

Within the palm groves a number of springs and pools are linked to underground *qanats* which distribute the water among the trees. Shady lanes lined with pomegranate bushes run among the trees, with little streams alongside them. So lush is the vegetation here that it is difficult to believe that the arid ridges of the burial mounds are less than a couple of kilometres away.

All along the coastline southwards from here are palm groves and plantations, elegant new villas and old fishing villages. These villages are in the process of transformation from clusters of traditional coral-built cottages to new breeze-block houses.

The first of the villages after the causeway is Jasra, a pretty village on the shore. Here the old village has been replaced by attractively designed modern houses lining the roadside. Only the old mosque remains of the former village, and a cottage or two, nicely repainted and fitting comfortably among the elegant new houses.

On the southern outskirts of this model village is the totally renovated traditional house in which the Amir, Shaikh Isa, was born. The house is now a museum, well furnished with the contemporary furnishings of 50 years ago. It boasts a bedroom, *majlis*, and kitchens, but is not large compared with many of the old palaces on the island. Perhaps because the rooms are small and so fully equipped, they must be viewed from the doorways, through sheet-glass panels.

Along the coast, opposite this house, are estates of the ruling family. The *qanat* which once watered them is still clearly visible, running at right angles to the road, alongside a small asphalted lane leading eastwards, a little to the south of Shaikh Isa's birthplace.

A line of *qanat* shafts beside the lane open on to a fairly deep *qanat* which still contains a little water in it. Clusters of lush green reeds grow out of some of the shafts and at the crossroads with the coast road on the western side of the road, is an access shaft with stone steps leading down into the *qanat*. Here in the past, the villagers would have come to collect sweet water, for the water from the wells in the village was brackish.

South of Jasra the villages are sited a little inland of the shore, close by the roadside. Al Hamala, the first of them, still has some appealing but abandoned old houses set among its palm groves. Then come the villages of Dumistan, Karzakkan, Malikiya and Sadad, now all slightly overshadowed by the vast urban development of Hamad Town on the ridge just to the east of them.

The next village right on the beach is Zellaq, on an attractive stretch of coastline which has long been a weekend favourite. Close by is the BAPCO beach and sailing club, one of the main centres for sailing in Bahrain.

The ancient cemetery at Sar was a major archaeological discovery.

Some qanats or irrigation channels are still visible today, like this one among the palm groves.

The traditional siyam, or summer sleeping platform, Beit Jasra.

A woman plaiting palm mats at the Al Jasra Handicraft Centre.

Zellaq village itself is happily situated on a wide bay, its waters brimming with small fibreglass fishing boats, while some larger wooden *dhows* swing at anchor a little further out. Before the completion of the causeway these *dhows* and many others plied back and forth to Saudi Arabia. Today their role has ended, unless they are used for a little fishing too.

At the northern end of the bay are the remains of a picturesque old house, built right at the water's edge beside a cluster of palm trees. This was the house of Abdullah Al Dousari, the secretary of Shaikh Hamad, the Amir's grandfather.

Beyond the village, large estates continue to line the seashore, until one reaches the splendid Al Jaza'ir beach, some seven kilometres further south.

This long beach has been developed as a leisure resort, with feathery tamarisk bushes planted down to the water's edge and palm-frond beach cabins offering shade and privacy. Beyond it one reaches the southern region for which permission to enter is required.

Areen Wildlife Sanctuary

Many of Zellaq's menfolk today work in the large Areen wildlife park which has been developed a little to the south of the village. Some of the young men have exchanged their hereditary fisherman's calling for a degree in zoology, to help run this ambitious project.

The park covers an area of eight square kilometres, extensively planted with indigenous desert trees for shade. Here antelopes, gazelle, wild sheep, ibex, oryx and ostrich roam at large, safe within the enclosure fence and fearing no predators, for the park houses only herbivores.

The project was started in 1976 by the Crown Prince, Shaikh Hamad, to conserve and shelter indigenous Arabian animals threatened with extinction.

A further impetus to its development was the dramatic plight of a number of zebras stranded at Rome airport in 1979. They were unclaimed, and when the Ruler heard about them he decided to give them a home. They, or their descendants, are still to be seen in the park.

Today, half the total area of the park is fenced off as a special reserve for these endangered species, and access is restricted.

In the other section of the park visitors are driven along small winding roads, among the animals who take little notice of cars and continue to graze close by the roadside. Since many of the creatures are breeding, young animals are often visible and even the majestic ostriches can be seen with their offspring.

Water for ablution and drinking, Beit Jasra.

Oryx in the Areen Wildlife Park were once indigenous to the region.

BAHRAIN – ISLAND HERITAGE

In ancient times ostriches roamed at large in Bahrain, for in the burial mounds their eggshells are often found, sometimes decorated for use as beakers. There have been no ostriches here however, nor in the rest of Arabia within living memory, which makes it a special pleasure to see them so at ease in Areen.

The Arabian oryx is another species which had become extinct throughout the whole peninsula, the last ones known in the wild were hunted down in 1974. Zoos and wildlife parks have made a special effort since then to re-establish the oryx in Arabia, starting with a few held in captivity.

Areen is making a notable contribution to this effort, and now has an impressive herd roaming freely in the reserve. These dramatic, black and white antelopes with their long, straight horns, are thought to be the origin of the legendary unicorn. They share their park with the *rhim* gazelle, which have fared better than other Arabian species and can still be seen living in the wild, in the south of the island.

Finally, the Areen park is working on those popular birds, the falcon and the *houbara*, or bustard, whose passage on migration through the peninsula causes such a wave of excitement. Here they breed and train the falcon, an arduous task since falcons bred in captivity are notoriously difficult to train, and they are attempting the challenge of breeding *houbara*.

The sanctuary offers a stimulating mix of safari park, scientific research and serious wildlife conservation. Visitors are introduced to its work by a video, before being taken on tour.

Above: Ostrich in the Areen Wildlife Park.
Right: A herd of camels grazing near Hamala.

WEST COAST

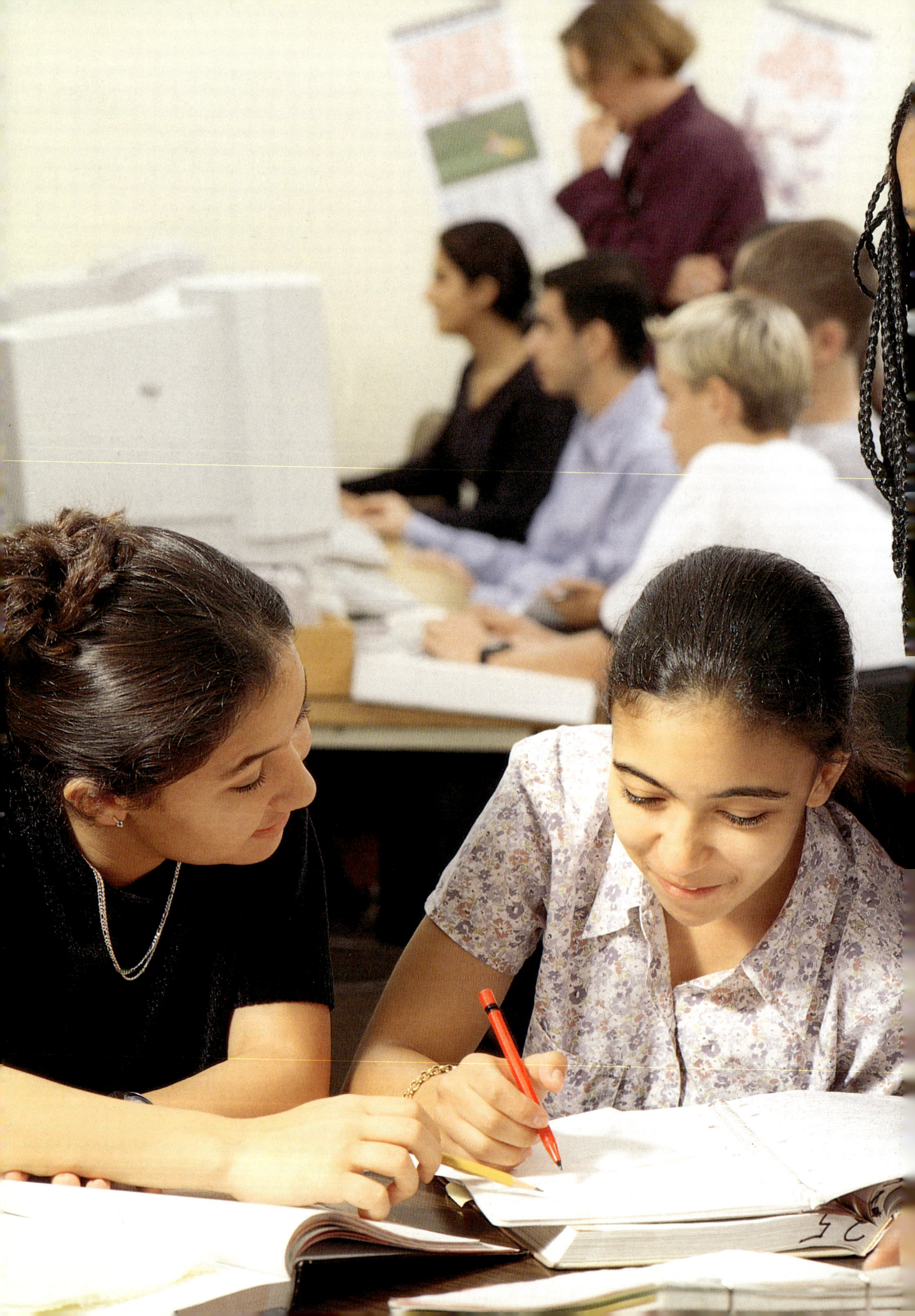

Chapter 9

TOWNSHIPS OF THE CENTRE

The twin towns of East and West Rifaa stand on the very edge of the rim rock, looking southwards over the great central depression of the island towards Awali and Jebel Dukhan. The site is a healthy one, higher and drier than most of the island, enjoying clear fresh air and free in the past of the malaria which troubled the inhabitants of the palm belt.

The Al Khalifas and their allies of the Utub tribe made this place their home when they first came to Bahrain in the late 18th century, and the old villages expanded until, by the start of this century, together they constituted the third largest town in the islands, following only Manama and Muharraq.

East Rifaa, the original home of the Al Khalifas, is by far the bigger of the two. The old part of the town still has much of the character of a traditional Bahraini settlement, with the singular exception of having a large oil pipeline running alongside the main street. This is the pipeline which brings oil from Saudi Arabia, under the sea and right across the island to the refinery. It carries, as it were, the very lifeblood of Bahrain.

The Al Khalifa Rulers made their home in the old fort on the edge of the cliff of East Rifaa. This fort was probably already 100 years old when the Al Khalifas took it, a picturesque place which dominates the low-lying ground between East and West Rifaa, where the best spring in the island is situated.

Down there, among a grove of acacia and palm trees, is the well of Ain Al Hunainiya. It has a strange, high superstructure which in the past enabled animals to draw up the water, but today it is worked by diesel pump and draped with pipework. So highly was this water rated that in the olden days it was carried by donkeys from here to Manama for the townspeople to drink.

Bahrain's educational institutions are mainly based in the townships, where the latest facilities to learn are available.

Modern minarets rise from behind burial mounds at Aali.

On the cliff above, a lone cannon standing beside the fort still points outwards towards this vital well. The owners of the fort needed to look to their own defence for it was at the centre of bitter struggles for power in the islands in the early part of the 19th century. The last shots in these disturbances were fired here at the fort, in 1869, when the Ruler, Shaikh Ali was killed there after only one year in power.

He was succeeded by his son, Shaikh Isa bin Ali, a young man only 21 years old, but whose rule was to be the longest, and most peaceful that Bahrain had known, and who was to live until the dawn of the oil age in 1932.

The fort of East Rifaa which he inherited was a fine building with some attractive stucco work still visible today. Mr and Mrs Bent, who visited the island at the end of the 19th century, left this description: "The Rifaa are much older than Moharek and Manameh, fortified villages with castellated walls of mud bricks. Here, many of the Al Khalifa family reside in comfortable houses. The courtyards of these houses are architecturally interesting: the Saracenic arch, the rosettes or openwork stucco... great boons in a hot land to let in the air without sun."

But Shaikh Isa eventually made his main home in the large and even more intricately decorated house in Muharraq, now known by his name, and the fort of Rifaa was left empty. Today it has been renovated and can be visited.

From the middle of the 20th century the Al Khalifa family has made its home in West Rifaa and transformed the place into a pleasant garden city. The roads are lined with shady trees while borders and roundabouts are filled with flowers. Shaikh Salman was the first to settle here, and has been followed by his son, Shaikh Isa, the Amir, and by his grandson Shaikh Hamad. Their homes represent the transformation in building styles in Bahrain over the past half-century.

THE ARAB HORSE

On the southern edge of West Rifaa, at the top of the cliff by the roadside, a modern tower building stands guard over a collection of fine horses tethered at its foot. They are part of the stables of the Al Khalifa family, horses which are heirs to a long tradition of careful breeding.

Gulf Arab horses have always been esteemed among the very best of the famous breed, and many used to make the journey by *dhow* – sharing space with a cargo of dates – to eager buyers in India.

The Al Khalifas brought their horses with them in the past when these animals were essential for desert warfare. Even when no longer needed for this purpose, the ruling family continued to breed their small fiery mounts, most of which were dark bays or greys.

In the 19th century some of the best of these horses were presented by the Rulers of the day to the Khedives

On parade before the race, Sakhir racecourse.

Mounted guard exercising.

of Egypt, noted fanciers of horseflesh. Later in the century, Lady Anne Blunt, a leading British expert on Arab horses, made a trip to Bahrain to buy for her own stables.

It was only with the rule of Shaikh Salman, in the 1940s, however, that horse-racing was introduced to Bahrain, first in Muharraq, then Manama, and finally at the old racecourse just below the rim rock to the south of West Rifaa. There, an oval track was laid out beneath the cliffs, and a large stable established.

An appreciative visitor to the track was Queen Elizabeth II of Great Britain on the occasion of a state visit to Bahrain, in 1979.

In 1981, however, a far more ambitious, grass racecourse was opened on the northern side of the Zellaq road, almost opposite the Sakhir palace. This complex covers 520 hectares and includes numerous stable blocks and a stand for 10,000 spectators. The Equestrian and Horse Racing Club holds races here during the winter season on Fridays.

Jockeys and racehorse owners are attracted from all over the world to Gulf racing, whose fame has grown in recent years by the institution of several prestigious prizes. The Dubai World Cup, held each year during the latter part of March, is, at the time of writing, the world's most valuable horse-race. The racing in Bahrain is to some extent a preparation for that, as well as a national event in its own right. Its chief race is the Crown Prince's Cup, also run in March.

View of the finish of a race at Sakhir racecourse, with Jebel Dukhan in the background.

Children of Aali playing among the burial mounds.

Kilns of Aali, built into the side of ancient burial mounds.

At the Sakhir racecourse the entrants will be from all sorts of stables, and the jockeys will be Bahraini, Irish, Pakistani, French and so on. The audience is a keen one, thoroughly knowledgeable about the points of each new season's mounts.

Bahrainis love horses and riding; a spirited Arab grey out for exercise with its owner is a common sight around the villages or under the ramparts of the Portuguese fort. Or you may come upon a posse of village boys riding bareback on equally fine, if less well-groomed, horses. The Bahrain Equestrian Association in Shakhurah is a focal point for many activities.

AALI

Major developments have taken place, too, in one of Bahrain's oldest settlements, the village of Aali in the very centre of the island. This must have been a place of great importance in ancient times, for here the island's largest burial mounds are found, a collection of huge, double-storey tumuli, up to 25 metres high, which were always considered to be 'the tombs of the kings'. Several of them were excavated in the last century and yielded a few fine objects now known to be typical grave offerings of the tombs built around 2000 BC. But all the Aali tombs had been extensively robbed in ancient times and their contents were but a token of what they must once have contained.

The villagers had always lived and worked in among these tombs, their stone-built houses being better than those of most other villages and sheltered among the great mounds. Aali was a large, active and prosperous village with flourishing potteries and a lime-burning industry. For both these occupations the craftsmen used the grave mounds as their kilns, building their furnaces up into the sides of the mounds and firing them with brushwood and palm-fronds.

These ancient crafts still flourish today, the potters spreading their mostly unglazed wares out in the sun beside their little workshops, the lime burners transforming piles of stone into fine white powder for use in making gypsum.

The potters have also set up a row of booths along the north side of the Wali al Ahed highway which runs east-west between Sitra and the turn to the causeway to Saudi Arabia, passing through the two Rifaas along its way.

As the village has prospered it has expanded with houses being built ever closer to the burial mounds whose edges have been eroded in the process. In some cases the earth mounds have been cut back to their surrounding stone ring wall which is clearly visible. In others the old cuttings of excavations of long ago reveal parts of the burial chambers, now silted up with fallen earth and litter.

Pottery from Aali and household goods displayed beside the Wali al Ahed highway.

On the eastern outskirts of the village some elegant modern villas have been built, while to the west stand the palm groves, and many smaller burial mounds.

Isa Town

Today Aali almost joins up with Isa Town, the 'new town' to the east of it. This town was a novel development for Bahrain, when it was built in the late 1960s, a town built from scratch in the desert to provide homes for Bahraini families, a town of modern houses with no historical roots, unlike the rest of the island's settlements.

The houses were designed with an Islamic feel, a pointed arch covering the recessed front door. They were painted in shades of brown, olive green and dull red, but today many of the inhabitants have repainted their own houses in white or cream. This town, which was first inhabited in 1968, was designed for 35,000 inhabitants.

Since its inauguration the town has attracted a number of government departments, notably the Traffic Directorate headquarters, the Ministry of Information, and the Bahrain Radio and Television broadcasting station as well as the Bahrain Cultural Centre where plays and concerts are held. It also became the seat of Bahrain's first college of higher education, the Gulf Technical College, which recently combined with the Gulf University College to become the University of Bahrain, on the southern outskirts of the town.

Isa Town gained another attraction when the huge National Stadium was opened a little to the south of the town in 1983. Numerous international football matches have been played there since its inauguration.

Although the original town was expanded by the addition of many apartment blocks around the outskirts,

Bahrain places great emphasis on education.

BAHRAIN – ISLAND HERITAGE

this still could not satisfy the pressing demand for accommodation for Bahrain's population which is rapidly expanding at the rate of 3.2 per cent per annum. A further dramatic step was therefore taken in the 1980s with the decision to construct yet another, totally new town a little further south and west.

Above: Schoolgirls of Hamad Town. Below: Hamad Town has made provision to equip schools and colleges with the latest in computer technology.

HAMAD TOWN

Hamad Town, named after the Crown Prince, Shaikh Hamad, lies between the Awali to Jasra road and the Awali to Zellaq road. It extends for some nine kilometres along the rim rock from north to south, but is rather narrow in proportion to its length. The town is built on arid, stony ground which was not suitable for agriculture, but which was the site of vast fields of ancient burial mounds.

Some areas of these burial mounds have been preserved and fenced off, close beside the new houses. Others were excavated before construction of the town and proved to contain among them some of the earliest burials of that type in Bahrain. They indicate that people had already settled in the region of Hamad Town some 4,500 years ago.

The town is built of square white houses with vertical bands of bright colours rising through the windows, which are capped with a half-moon design of traditional carved stucco work. Striking pinks, blues and yellows enliven an otherwise monochrome scene of white houses in a pale landscape, as yet unrelieved by much vegetation. The goal is for 5,000 houses which the inhabitants can buy gradually over the years as they live there.

The town is arranged in neighbourhood districts and the planners have avoided the pitfall of a rigid grid pattern. Here the streets run in natural curves following the hillsides, relieving the impression of stark newness. Already some of the inhabitants are beginning to add their own touch to their homes, a different wall or porch for example, while around the outside of the town individually owned and designed villas are going up. The civic status of this new town is marked on its southern border by a monumental gateway bearing the coat of arms of the State of Bahrain.

Immediately to the south of Hamad Town, and opposite it on the other side of the Awali to Zellaq road, are the impressive new buildings of the Bahrain University. This sumptuous complex of grey concrete buildings, grouped around the soaring minaret of the university mosque was originally designed for the Arabian Gulf University by the famous Japanese architect, Kenzo Tange. The approach roads are lined with flowering bougainvillaea, fountains cool the air of the entrance courtyard, the quiet corridors of the administrative building are comfortably carpeted and the walls covered with a tasteful blue-grey suede finish.

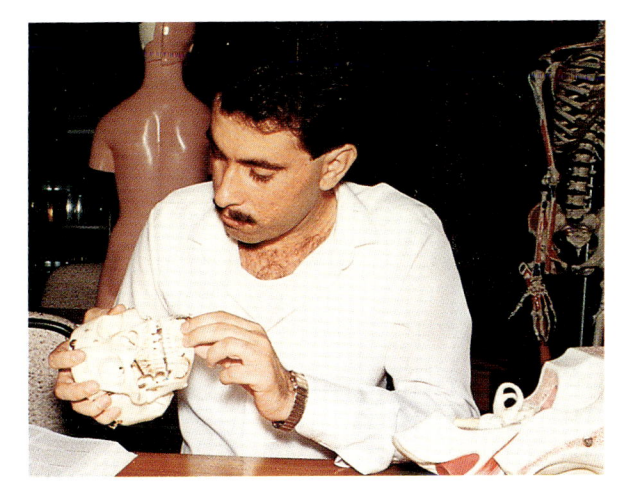

A medical student in a well-equipped laboratory on the university campus.

The campus was commissioned and built by the AGCC countries and Iraq, as a regional centre for post-graduate research, largely concentrating on the sciences, and was designed to accommodate 5,000 students. It covers an area of four million square metres and its clean-lined modern buildings are grouped around a wide central courtyard. Facilities include a large auditorium with a seating capacity of 1,500, a smaller conference hall for seminars and conferences, an open-air theatre and a magnificent library. In this splendid campus, set in the open desert, Bahrain's students can already enjoy a taste of the world of the 21st century.

The imposing Gateway of Hamad Town.

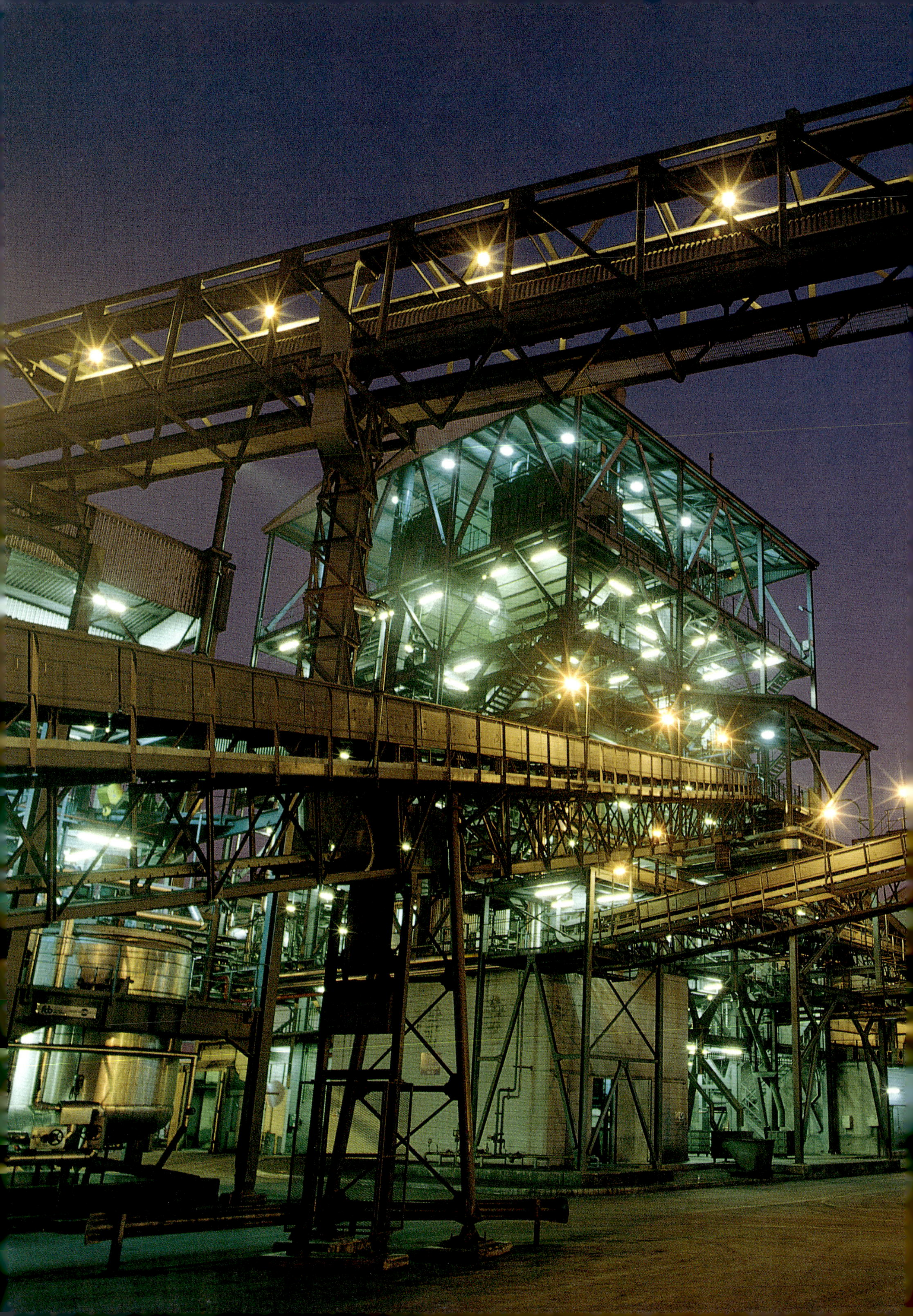

Chapter 10

THE INDUSTRIAL EAST COAST

The shallow waters which surround the islands of Bahrain give way on the east coast to some deep-water channels coming close into shore. It was here that the first major steps in the development of the country took place; initially with the construction, in the 1930s, of the oil refinery and the oil-loading terminal off Sitra island, and subsequently in the early 1950s with the construction of the first modern harbour of Mina Sulman near Jufair.

For 4,000 years Bahrain had flourished as a maritime trading nation using simple shallow-draft *dhow* harbours, of which the first had been the open roadstead off the Bahrain fort. There the island's earliest merchant traders had found, and perhaps improved, a natural channel through the coral reef, which enabled their small craft to come in close to shore. By the 13th century the deep-water harbour of Arad bay on Muharraq island was also being used. But by the mid-20th century such simple harbours no longer sufficed, a major commercial port was needed.

The Mina Sulman port, constructed on the north-east corner of Bahrain island, soon proved its worth and was considerably expanded in the early 1960s and again, even more extensively, in the mid-1970s. Then a large container terminal was developed, linked to a major industrial area for light industries.

In 1977 another dock was built some five kilometres out to sea, due east of Mina Sulman and taking advantage of the same deep-water channel. This was a dry dock, the Arab Shipbuilding and Repair Yard (ASRY), which was built on an artificial island. Although it is approached by causeway from Hidd on Muharraq island, it is actually only a couple of kilometres across the water from the oil and aluminium terminals, which are linked by jetty, to Sitra island. Large tankers and merchant ships plying the

A sophisticated network at ALBA's Carbon Department.

Natural spring on Nabih Salih island, in its former glory during the 1980s.

The sea offers an important leisure resource for tourists and locals.

waters of the northern Gulf can easily come into this dock for repair and refit.

ASRY's dry dock was greatly expanded in the early 1990s. It has proved to be one of the most important revenue earners of the island. As one of the few fully-equipped big-ship repair yards between the Mediterranean and Singapore this is understandable. At the same time a large new container port was initiated, close to the south Hidd industrial area, with extensive container storage facilities, to complement those at Mina Sulman.

COASTAL ISLANDS

Although the prosperity of the east coast has stemmed from its deep-water access, the prevailing impression of this region is nevertheless one of shallow waters with fishermen wading far out from the shore in water only up to their waists, wielding hand nets or tending their fish traps. This is because the coast of Bahrain island is deeply indented in this north-east section by the shallow lagoon Khor Al Kabb, almost closed off from the sea by the long, low outline of Sitra island.

One of the most bizarre accidents in the nation's recent history happened in this area back in 1950. On a stormy night an Air France plane coming in from Indonesia crashed in the sea off Sitra. Two nights later, police and officials could hardly believe it when they were called out to another, identical crash. In completely calm weather, a second Air France plane from Indonesia had gone down in exactly the same place as the first. The reason why was never established.

In the centre of the bay floats the little island of Nabih Salih. This was once purely a fishing island, approached only by boat. Today, however, it has been linked by causeway to both the main island of Bahrain and to Sitra, and modern villas have been built among its palm trees. It was always a lush green island, drawing its water from two powerful springs, Ain Al Safahiya and Khawkab Ash Shaikh. However, like most other natural springs on Bahrain, these two are now virtually dry.

The village is named after the renowned *nabih* (holy man) Salih, whose mausoleum is housed in a renovated building first erected in 1446. Palm groves were the outstanding features of the island but sadly now the blackened stumps of many of the trees are witness to the depleted water levels. However, in spite of many changes the island still retains a special character, with a country feel to the old village, and its tiny ancient mosque, rather the worse for wear, balancing on a little mound, where its predecessors stood before.

The larger Sitra island, due east of Nabih Salih, was also once a place of palm groves and fishermen, but has

The old village of Nabih Salih.

The Gulf Petrochemical Industries plant.

Children enjoying the Bandar Club beach.

Jazirat-Al-Sheikh, a tiny island opposite Askar.

Catamaran from the Sitra island sailing club.

been greatly changed in modern times and now has a somewhat desolate appearance, with many of its palm trees dead and abandoned. The villages here have been greatly enlarged with recent housing and now tend to merge one into another.

The major change, however, has come from the extensive industrialisation of the island, which started in the late 1930s with the choice of its area for the oil terminal and storage depot. Now the north coast of the island houses the power station, a desalination plant and Bahrain Aluminium Extrusion Company, the narrow 'waist' of the island is occupied by vast round storage tanks for oil, while the Gulf Petrochemical Industries plant seems almost to float on the water on a little promontory of reclaimed land on the eastern side.

This plant produces ammonia and methanol for export throughout the world, and its capacity has recently been increased to 1,342 from 1,000 tonnes per day of each product. A urea plant is being added to the complex, with a capacity of 1,700 tonnes a day.

It is the extreme south of Sitra, however, which affords the most complete industrial vistas, which have a strange and unexpected beauty of their own. On Bahrain island, divided from Sitra here only by a narrow sea channel, stand the huge oil refinery and the aluminium smelter, almost side by side. At nightfall, from Sitra, the refinery is silhouetted against the setting sun, its fretted outline picked out by sparkling lights which are reflected in the waters of the creek. Swinging high above these waters are the cable-car buckets carrying alumina from the marine terminal out at sea to the aluminium smelter, and locked in perpetual motion. The high pylons carrying the cable cars march out to sea in straight, unbroken lines, a world away from the fishermen wading patiently through the shallows beneath them.

On the eastern coast of this southern part of the

THE INDUSTRIAL EAST COAST

Barasti huts are now rare; this one is near Jaaw.

island a row of very different little harbours adds a touch of colour and vitality to this industrial landscape. Northernmost of these is the *dhow* harbour of Bandar Al Dar run by the Directorate of Fisheries. Here rows of *dhows* are tied up at the quays, while little fishing boats come and go with their daily catch. It is one of the most picturesque harbours of the islands, and a good place to look for the freshest of fresh fish.

At the southern tip of the island is the sailing club's harbour, the source of fleets of brightly coloured sails propelling dinghies, yachts and catamarans out across the sheltered waters to the open sea beyond.

Between these two extremes is the marina and pleasure beach of the Bandar Club. This pleasant club boasts what must be the prettiest beach on the island, a crescent of fine golden sand sheltered from the sea by a small artificial island planted with full-grown palm trees. A well-situated restaurant and club facilities stand just above the beach and there are chalets, a swimming pool and tennis courts in the grounds.

Bauxite terminal off Sitra.

ALBA cable cars cross the evening sky, with the refinery in the background.

Workers of ALBA fabricating a crucible.

The Heavy Industries

Bahrain's two major industries stand on the shoulder of the main island, linked up with Sitra by causeway, oil pipeline and aluminium cable cars. These massive industrial projects, the refinery and the aluminium smelter, were each the first of their kind to be established in Arabia and have played a key role in the employment and training of young Bahrainis for an industrial future.

The refinery was opened in 1936. Almost from its inception, the refinery served Saudi Arabia's eastern oilfields as well as those of Bahrain, and some 80 per cent of its crude oil still comes from Saudi Arabia. Until 1997 the refinery was owned and operated by BAPCO, a joint venture company between the Government of Bahrain and Caltex. It is now wholly owned by the Government of Bahrain. The drying up of the oilfields early in the 21st century has long been foreseen, and the activities of the refinery and of ALBA will compensate for the loss. In the late 1960s, during a period of under-employment in Bahrain, an aluminium smelter Aluminium Bahrain (ALBA) was commissioned to absorb some of the surplus labour. The smelter made economic sense too, since it was part way between Australia, the source of the bauxite from which aluminium is made, and the markets of the West. Furthermore, it could make use of the ready supplies of gas from Bahrain's Khuff field.

Over the years the Bahrain Government increased its share in the smelter to a majority holding, and the Saudi Government also took a share. The capacity of the smelter has also been significantly enlarged and it is now the second largest in the world.

A substantial quantity of the smelter's output of aluminium is further processed in Bahrain, by the Gulf Aluminium Rolling Mills Company sited near the refinery, the Bahrain Aluminium Extrusion Company, Middle East Aluminium Cables and Bahrain Atomisers International. The rolling mills, officially opened in November 1986, now take a large amount of rolling ingot from ALBA each year.

Beyond ALBA the road continues southward along the east coast to the fishing villages of Askar and Jaaw. Here the industrial area ends, apart from the huge rock quarries on the inner cliff of the rim rock inland of these villages and facing the Jebel Dukhan. Jaaw is the nearest point of Bahrain to the town of Zubara on the Qatar coast, from which the Al Khalifa family set out for Bahrain. In the past century many of the inhabitants fled from Zubara and settled in Jaaw.

The tranquillity of this section of the eastern shoreline may not last for very long. Despite the construction of Isa Town and Hamad Town, many young

Oil storage tanks on Sitra island.

Bahrainis are still in need of a home of their own. If the demand for housing continues to be as pressing, and the rate of increase of the national population as rapid as ever, the next new town will be built in this region, to the south of ALBA. And this new town will also be the biggest of them all.

Transferring molten metal.

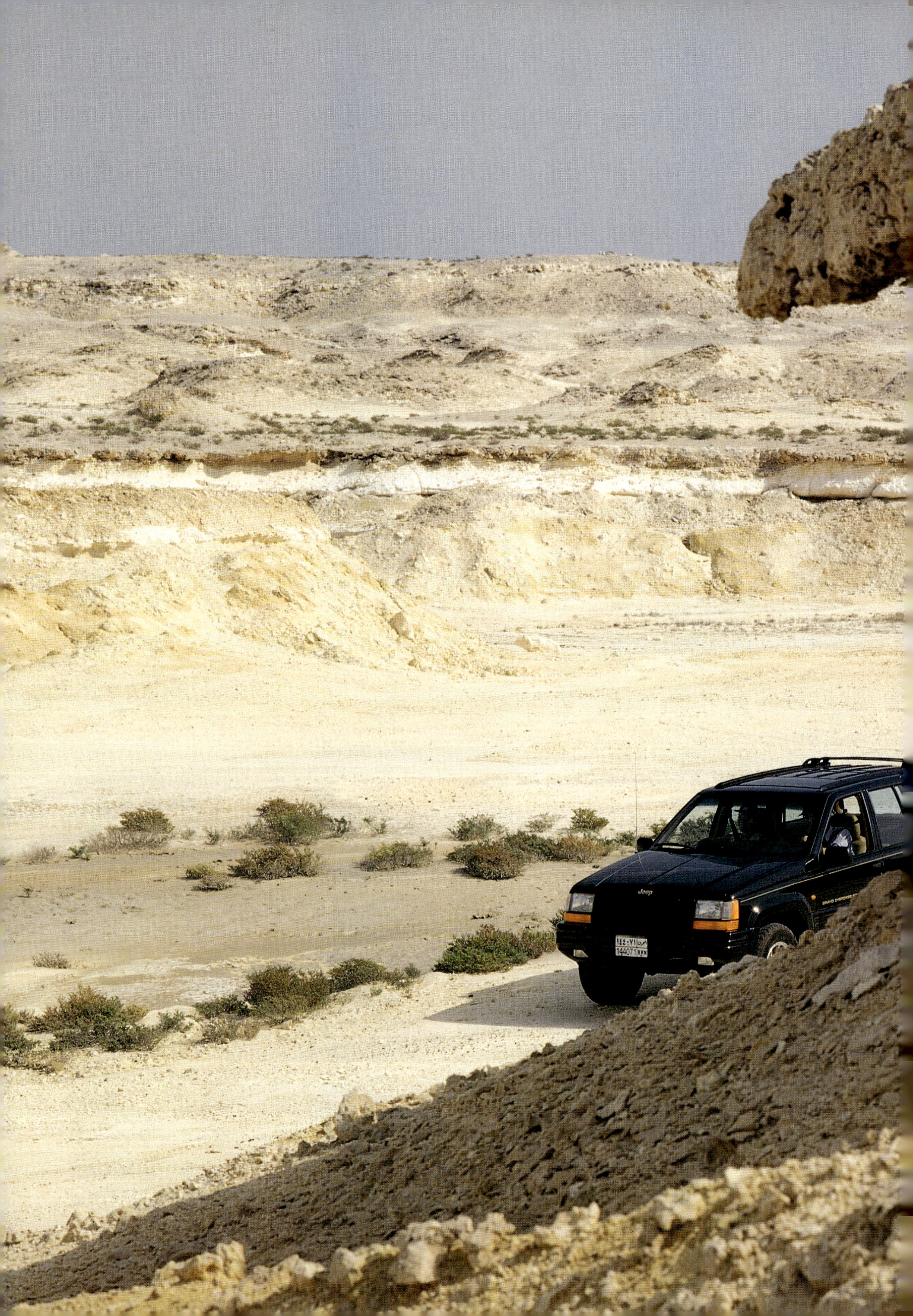

Chapter 11

MOUNTAIN AND MIRAGE

Nobody would really call the Jebel Dukhan a mountain, although that is what the word *jebel* actually means. In fact it is rather more of a hillock, a ridge of crumbling rock rising abruptly from a great oval depression. Nevertheless, its summit commands an impressive view out across the island and the sea beyond, and over to the mainland of Arabia on a clear day.

Its potential was recognised more than a century ago by Captain Durand who wrote of it: "From the top of the Jebel Dukhan, or hill of smoke, in the very centre of the larger island, a perfect view... is obtainable, and this if necessary, could be very easily made use of as a signalling station, as the hilltop is distinctly visible both from Muharrak and Manameh." Today the hilltop is indeed crowned by the large aerial dish of the tropospheric scatter station which forms part of Bahrain's telecommunications transmission network.

For all its present aridity, the area was once under water, as fossils of shellfish lying on the surface of the desert must indicate. So clearly defined are some of these 'shells' that it is difficult to believe they are made of stone. But the marine past brought more than shellfish to these shores. In the early 20th century Lorimer noted that a small deposit of asphalt penetrated the rocks five kilometres to the south-southeast of the *jebel*. At the time this was not taken to have much significance.

Today, however, all around Jebel Dukhan, the desert is criss-crossed with a maze of metal pipes running out over the sands like some giant spider's web. They bring in the oil from myriad well-heads, each marked by a column of valves and small wheels, or by one of the characteristic 'nodding donkey' pumps.

Two or three of these pumps have in recent times been given a fanciful character of their own. To the west

Off-road driving is popular in the Jebel Dukhan area.

Bahrain's oil industry stresses the process of refining.

Well near Sakhir Palace decorated to look like a hoopoe.

of the *jebel*, near the palace of Sakhir, is a nodding hoopoe, a realistic representation of the bird of passage whose arrival brightens the islands for a few months each year, while over on the eastern side, near the refinery, a lively yellow 'giraffe' nods in permanent motion.

Narrow asphalt lanes also create their own mesh-like network across the great central depression around the *jebel*. Follow one and as often as not it will end at a wellhead. They have an old-world atmosphere, these narrow roads, with their broken surface and sandy edges, ambling across the stony undulations. Yet they were laid down barely half a century ago.

Before that time the *jebel* and its desert were as undisturbed as they had been in the days of Lorimer, or for that matter as in the days of the builders of the burial mounds along the rim rock to the west. However, the year 1925, when the first oil concession was signed, was to hail fundamental change for Bahrain.

It was the summer when a terrible storm, harbinger of doom for the pearling industry, sank much of the diving fleet with great loss of life, so that for years afterwards men would refer to it as 'the year of the sinking'. And it was the year when Shaikh Hamad, who had recently replaced his aged father Shaikh Isa as Ruler of Bahrain, employed a young Englishman, Charles Belgrave, as his adviser to help him guide Bahrain into the modern world.

Both Charles Belgrave, and his son James, who was the first English baby to be born in Bahrain, were to spend the whole of their working lives there, and both left interesting accounts of the islands in their time.

The elderly Shaikh Isa had become Ruler of Bahrain back in 1869, when he was only 21 years old, and he ruled for 55 years. In his old age, however, he could not envisage a changed world and it was to fall to his son to encourage the difficult search for oil. Finally oil was struck in 1932, the year in which Shaikh Isa died at the age of 84. The first well to produce oil was dug at the southern foot of Jebel Dukhan and although it produced only modest quantities, it has been given full honours and is today painted in the national colours of red and white, and is adorned with a flag and a plaque.

It was only at the end of that year, however, that the Ruler and his adviser could rest assured that a genuine oil strike had been made. On a bitingly cold Christmas Day, Belgrave was called out to the *jebel*: "When Marjorie and I reached the well, which was in the foothills near Jebel Dukhan, we saw great ponds of black oil and black rivulets flowing down the wadis. Oil, and what looked to us like smoke, but which was in fact gas, spouted gustily from the drilling rig and all the machinery and the men who were working were dripping with oil... I could see, without any doubt that there was an oilfield in Bahrain."

Suburban lane in Awali.

AWALI AND NEIGHBOURHOOD

The oilmen lived at first in a temporary camp at the foot of the *jebel*. But as more wells were drilled and more workers arrived a more permanent home was needed. They chose a piece of rising ground, to the north-east of the *jebel*, which caught the passing breezes, and built a little township there. The place has a notably Western air. Rows of neat bungalows with sloping roofs line wide avenues shaded by trees. Brightly-coloured bougainvillaea, oleander and railway creeper tumble over the garden walls and children play outside with their bicycles.

The town was equipped with a cinema, social club, hospital and school and developed as a self-contained community. There was much debate, however, as to what to call the place, until in 1938 Shaikh Hamad chose a name: Awali. The name was apt, for it means 'high place' and furthermore it had been the name of the island in medieval times. The Arab geographer Idrisi wrote in 1154: "The principal island of Bahrain is Awal, six miles in length and breadth. Its capital is Bahrain, a populous town, the environs of which are fertile and produce grass and dates in abundance."

When it was first built, Awali was the most modern and cosmopolitan place on the island. In the late 1960s it still impressed with its garden-city atmosphere of another world. Today, however, the place is remarkable for having preserved exactly its appearance of those years, while all else around it has changed, often beyond recognition.

At the time Awali was built, Shaikh Hamad, to whom it owes its name and very existence, lived not far away, in the palace of Sakhir on the other side of the *jebel*. This palace stands alone, just to the south of the Awali-Zellaq road, and after Shaikh Hamad's death it was abandoned and stood empty for 40 years or so.

It was there that Charles Belgrave went, one night in 1925, to meet his future employer, and he described it thus: "The Shaikh's house, in the foothills, was a straggling group of buildings standing whitely in the desert without a vestige of vegetation around it. My impression of the place that night was that there were animals everywhere... We sat down on the carpeted floor in the *majlis* – reception room... it was 40 feet long but rather narrow... the walls of the room were decorated in arabesques cut in the plaster... We leant against large hard cushions, in white covers."

Sakhir Palace in the process of renovation.

BAHRAIN – ISLAND HERITAGE

The Tree of Life.

Today, the palace (which is not open) has changed little. It has recently been well renovated and shines starkly white, alone still in the desert though now there are a few acacia trees to shade the flocks and herds. And if one looks westwards from the palace, the architectural outlines of Bahrain University's modern buildings crown the distant ridge.

The only other building near the *jebel* is equally modern and just as striking. It is the treatment plant of Banagas, the Bahrain National Gas Company, which nestles at the eastern foot of Jebel Dukhan. Bahrain's oil was always associated with gas, as Belgrave's description shows, but until the 1980s nothing was done about it. Production had increased to 165 million standard cubic feet of gas per day in the late 1980s, increasing to more than 250 million cubic feet in the 1990s. Banagas is 75 per cent owned by the Bahrain Government, with Caltex and Apicorp sharing the remaining interest.

Camel herdsman with mother and baby in the late 1950s.

The Dhub lizard reaches 80cm in length.

Modern life seems far away from the sandy spit of Ras Al Barr at the southern tip of the island.

SOUTH OF THE JEBEL

The great oval depression in the centre of Bahrain is entirely bare of vegetation to the south of the *jebel*, except for a scatter of small desert shrubs on which herds of camels graze. Or almost entirely. A solitary great tree stands majestically alone some eight kilometres to the south-east of the *jebel*. This huge acacia (see page 102) is the more noticeable in that it is perched on a steep hillock, its great branches spreading out from a massive trunk to cover an area 25 metres across.

This notable landmark has earned the name of the Tree of Life, an appropriate title for it survives in an area of complete aridity. Yet the key to its existence may lie in the hillock beneath it, a mound covered with old potsherds and pieces of broken stone. In the past clearly it was the site of a settlement, an impression confirmed by the presence of a small Islamic cemetery of simple standing stones on a spur of the hillock to the north. Did the people who lived here in times gone by sink a deep well, one wonders, and might the tree have discovered the secret of the well to nourish its roots?

Beyond the tree the depression continues southwards until it is bounded by an abrupt cliff to the rim rock which then drops to a low plain and salt flats to the south. An asphalt road crosses the rim rock on both the east and the west sides, but beyond this point the south of the island is a restricted military area and permission to enter is needed.

Even before the days of military development, the south of the island was restricted as it was the hunting ground of the Shaikh. On the western side, two charming little old hunting lodges stand witness to those times. They were a favourite retreat of Shaikh Hamad who by chance died here in the lodge of Rumaitha when he suffered a sudden stroke in 1942.

It was a peaceful place to have spent the last days of his life. Outside, small Arabian gazelles still roam in the wild, huge *dhub* lizards bask in the sun like strange antediluvian monsters, and pink flamingoes wade in the shallows of lagoons along the shore. Some of the oldest traces of man's presence in the islands have been found along this south-west coast, in the form of scatters of shells, flint instruments, and tiny pieces of pottery, made in Al Ubaid in Iraq some 6,000 years ago.

Herds of camels roam this section of the desert, and it is not uncommon to see gazelles grazing alongside them. So unafraid was one baby gazelle that it only took to its heels when the camel herd walked right up to it. Even the adults stand and watch an approaching vehicle, quite undisturbed, and only run off with a flick of the tail when the vehicle draws close.

As one travels south the desert becomes more arid

Grazing and pumping in the shadow of the western rim rock.

and drops imperceptibly to extensive salt flats along the southern shore. Mirages of intense clarity flicker across the salt flats, confusing reality, so that it is hard to tell whether the sea is in front or behind. The asphalt road from the east side of the island runs right down to a little coastguard station, some 32 kilometres south of ALBA and only six kilometres from the southernmost point of the island; on the west side of the island the asphalt has come to an end long before.

The southern tip of the island runs out into a narrow spit of sand, a kilometre long, at Ras Al Barr. This strip of sand, only a few metres across, points out to sea, towards Saudi Arabia, and is fringed with shallow beaches. Along its western edge are a line of old fish traps in the clear, aquamarine water. Modern life seems far away.

Yet it was precisely this quiet desert region south of the *jebel* which launched Bahrain on the path of extensive development – a development which was to lead to the high-rise architecture of the Diplomatic Quarter in Manama, the two universities, and the sophisticated urban society of the capital. The old grazing and hunting preserves actually held a much richer treasure, noted by Lorimer, and used in ancient times to make boats and baskets watertight. Those telltale seepages of asphalt from the pale coloured rocks near the *jebel* were to herald the dawn of a new age.

Cormorants perching on a sea marker.

106

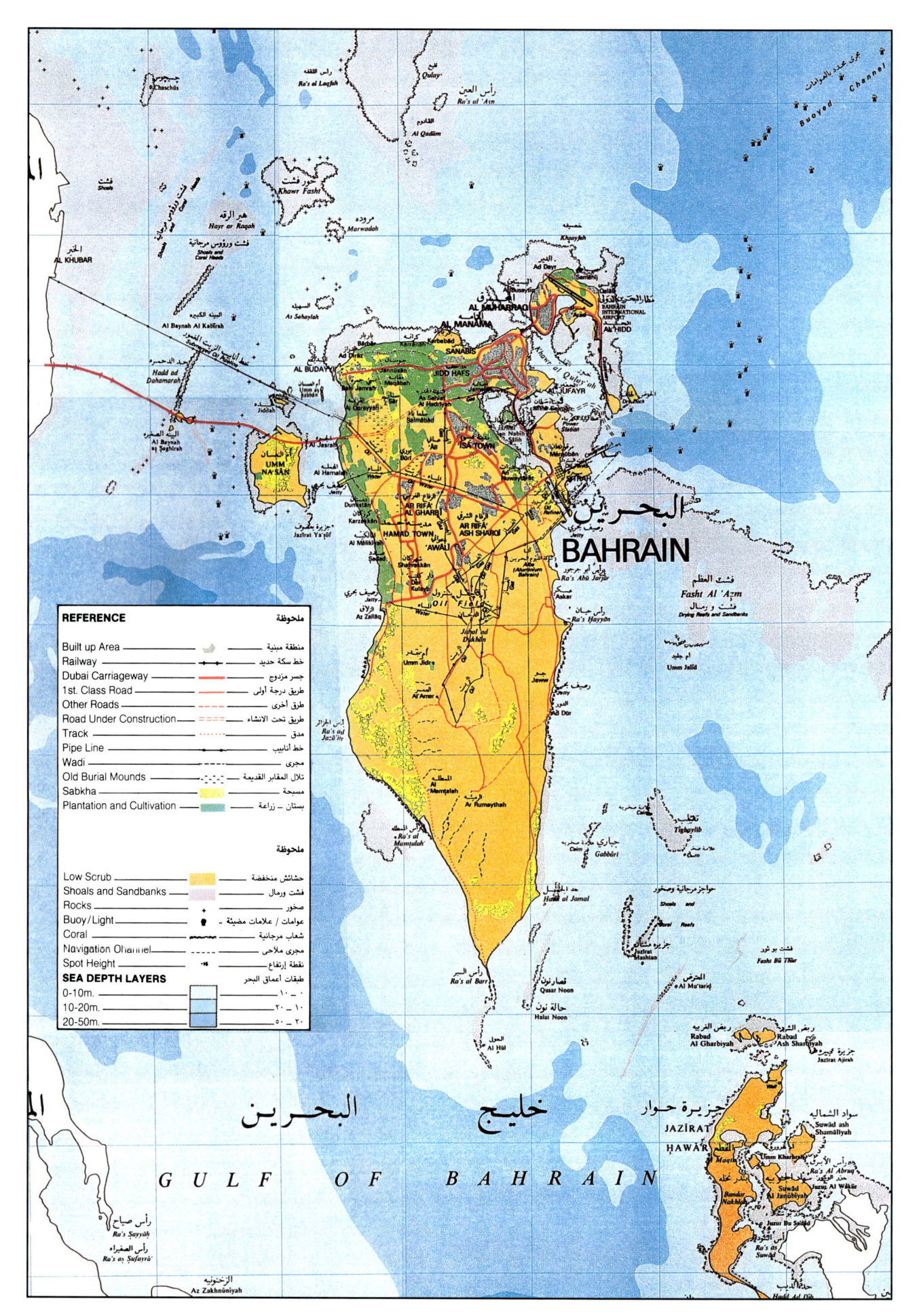

TOURISM IN BAHRAIN

The tourist is not only welcome in Bahrain, he is actively courted by government and inhabitants alike. Indeed tourism is probably Bahrain's fastest-growing industry and now employs more people than the country's basic oil and aluminium industries.

Every facility exists, whether man-made or natural, to give the visitor a comfortable stay. The capital is exceedingly well-equipped with first class hotels; the following pages introduce The Diplomat Hotel,

The portico of the Siyadi mosque is a delightful example of traditional design.

Gulf Hotel, Bahrain Hilton, Holiday Inn Bahrain, Le Royal Meridien and Sheraton Bahrain. Excursions are readily available to the many tourist sights both within and around the capital.

The 25-kilometre causeway linking Bahrain with Saudi Arabia has proved the biggest single factor in attracting visitors to the various islands. Bahrain is equally popular with visitors arriving by air. The island lies on many of the major east-west airline routes. It is a good place to break the journey for a few days, or longer, and enjoy the climate, particularly in winter. Today, more and more visitors, who perhaps first experienced Bahrain in that way, are now making the islands their primary holiday destination in the sun.

Another advantage that Bahrain has to offer is its size. The island is so compact that no one needs to undertake a long journey: all the interesting sights are within an hour's drive of the capital and a detailed tour of any one region can comfortably be made in half a day.

For those with an interest in history, ancient burial sites abound throughout the islands and much can be learned from the splendid museum in Manama. From the more recent past, forts and palaces which a few years ago were crumbling ruins, have now been restored by the government and are open to the public. The visitor can savour the lifestyle of the 19th century ruler and his merchants, or walk the battlements of the 15th century Portuguese fort.

The islands also have many contemporary attractions in the burgeoning modern cities and these too should not be missed if the visitor truly wants to appreciate this attractive island state.

Visitors can enjoy bargaining in the pottery souqs.

THE DIPLOMAT HOTEL

The Diplomat Hotel, part of Forte and Le Meridien Hotel Group, is located in the city centre of Manama city. Its 243 rooms and suites all have spectacular views over the Arabian Gulf.

Guest rooms have the latest amenities, including direct dial telephones, satellite television, fax and computer facilities. In addition to the range of standard and superior rooms, hotel guests can enjoy the Royal Club, the hotel's own executive floor. Royal Club members benefit from exclusive privileges such as a separate breakfast buffet area, afternoon tea, complimentary cocktails, and airport transfers. The Club rooms located on the tenth and eleventh floors of the hotel have recently been completely refurbished.

The hotel's range of restaurants and bars is extensive. The Veneziano is traditionally Italian with a pizza oven at its centre, while The Fiddler's Green Irish restaurant has a unique Gaelic atmosphere. Twenty four-hour dining is offered by the Al Warah's international buffets which promote different themes almost every evening. In addition, the lively Al Fanar nightclub on the fourteenth floor features popular Arabic entertainers as well as European dancers. In contrast, the Skylight lounge offers a tranquil and secluded setting in which to enjoy cocktails while overlooking Manama and the island of Muharraq.

The banqueting suite can accommodate 1,800 guests.

The Diplomat Hotel offers a wide choice of leisure facilities. Le Mirage Health Club has been totally upgraded and offers two gyms, for men and women, two flood-lit tennis courts, two air-conditioned squash courts and a temperature-controlled outdoor swimming pool. For younger guests there is the exciting Penguin Village with its playground and castle.

The impressive banqueting suite can cater for events for as many as 1,800 guests, with the Grand Ambassador Suite offering state-of-the-art sound and lighting systems. Smaller venues are also available with private dining-rooms.

The Diplomat Hotel is now firmly established in the market as a five-star business and leisure hotel.

The Diplomat Hotel has an impressive façade.

GULF HOTEL

The Gulf Hotel plays a prominent role in welcoming visitors to Bahrain, offering superb comfort and service.

In the heart of the Gulf lies the most established hotel in Bahrain – the Gulf Hotel. In 1967, reclamation was carried out on a small peninsula of land and developed into a site for the Gulf Hotel, which today celebrates 30 years of hospitality service. Conveniently located only five minutes from the city centre and 10 minutes from Bahrain International Airport, the hotel is regarded by many as the best choice for business and pleasure.

The hotel offers high standards throughout, and in each of its 366 luxurious rooms the latest amenities are available, including interactive television. Direct online access to the Internet and e-mail information services are among many other features that help to make each room a mini business centre for individual guests. In addition, the Gulf Hotel boasts a fully-equipped business centre, complete with adjoining conference rooms that provide state-of-the-art technical equipment and professional assistance.

A convenient shopping arcade in the hotel includes an airline reservation office, ladies' and men's hairdressers, boutique, gift shop, jewellery shop and newsagent, not forgetting a pastry shop and delicatessen.

There is a wide selection of restaurants, offering superb quality in dining. Connoisseurs of Italian cuisine may choose La Pergola, while Zahle offers the best in Lebanese food. Guests can dine out in Oriental style, enjoying a choice of Pekinese or Cantonese or Szechuan at the China Garden restaurant; if Sushi Sashimi is the preference of the evening, the hotel's Japanese restaurant Sato will satisfy guests' appetites.

Meanwhile, Al Waha Cafe restaurant provides international cuisine twenty-four hours a day. For panoramic views of Bahrain, the rooftop Stars Lounge is a memorable experience, while the Sherlock Holmes English Tavern is the ideal retreat in which to relax to live entertainment. The Palm Grove Lounge offers a quiet ambience with entertainment.

The Gulf Hotel plays host to many international events. The Gulf International Convention Centre is a showcase of professionalism, offering every facility and resource support for mounting every type of event, and to the highest standards. The GICC offers 9,575 square metres of ballroom, meeting and public areas, with state-of-the-art facilities, and has the added flexibility to cater for as little as 10 or up to 2,200 people.

The aim of the Men's and Women's Health Clubs is to create a holistic well-being for all those wishing to participate in the fitness facilities and relaxation treatments. Each offers the latest apparatus in the form of a fully-equipped gym, sauna, Jacuzzi and steam room. The two flood-lit tennis courts, two air-conditioned squash courts and a large temperature-controlled swimming pool complete the expansive range of facilities at the Gulf Hotel.

A choice of luxurious rooms awaits discerning guests.

Al Murjan – the Gulf International Convention Centre.

BAHRAIN HILTON

The Bahrain Hilton benefits from a central location.

The Bahrain Hilton is ideally located in the heart of the new commercial and diplomatic area in Manama, within easy walking distance of the main shopping area and just five kilometres from the International Exhibition Centre and only eight kilometres from the international airport.

First of the international chain hotels on the island, it opened in 1976. The Hilton houses 250 rooms, including luxury suites, all of which have the latest facilities. The hotel was the first to introduce the executive floor concept, offering superior accommodation for the business traveller, with its executive lounge providing complimentary breakfast, pre-lunch and dinner canapés and beverages. A fully-equipped business centre is available.

The hotel's conference and banqueting facilities cater for seminars, shows, banquets and conventions. The Gilgamesh Ballroom or the Executive Meeting Room with in-built audio-visual equipment can accommodate business meetings plus two smaller boardrooms.

Local and international cuisine can both be sampled at the Hilton: restaurants range from the Al Wasmeyyah 24-hour coffee shop, the elegant Grill, to the Kei Japanese restaurant and the Al Bustan Club. The Cavalry Club Lounge provides a meeting place with an English atmosphere and live entertainment.

The Al Sawani Restaurant serves a medley of Middle Eastern dishes.

The Bahrain Hilton also operates the unique Al Sawani Restaurant, which was built by the Ministry of Tourism and opened in May 1992. Located by the National Museum, this restaurant's architectural style is reminiscent of Andalusian castles and Damascene palaces with a blend of traditional Arabian Gulf themes. Open daily for both lunch and dinner, serving a mixture of traditional Middle Eastern dishes, along with live nightly entertainment. The hotel offers complimentary transport to and from the restaurant upon request.

There is no shortage of recreation facilities at the Hilton; in addition to its temperature-controlled swimming pool there is a health club with a sauna, mini-gym, hot and cold plunge-pools, table tennis, games room and two flood-lit tennis courts. Other hotel facilities include hairdressing and beauty salons, pastry shop, gift shop and car rental agency.

The Grill is a popular dining venue.

The temperature-controlled swimming pool.

HOLIDAY INN BAHRAIN

Only five minutes from the International Airport, the Holiday Inn Bahrain enjoys a central location, within easy walking distance of Manama's commercial centre, major shopping areas, the souq, and popular tourist attractions. The hotel combines modern business facilities with a relaxed resort atmosphere to cater for the diverse needs of business travellers and holiday visitors to the island.

The hotel's five-star status is reflected throughout the 275 well-appointed bedrooms which are all equipped with the latest amenities. In addition, the superior Executive floors offer deluxe accommodation, with a further choice of single, executive, Royal suites and non-smoking rooms.

Dining facilities include the Al Maharah Restaurant offering fresh seafood and themed buffets; the Al Dar coffee-shop open 24 hours; The Peak Restaurant serving light refreshments; an international nightclub, and the Harvesters Lounge, a popular venue for live entertainment and casual family dining.

For the energetic, the Nautilus Fitness Centre offers state-of-the-art exercise equipment, supervised by qualified instructors, complete with sauna, Jacuzzi and massage room for relaxation. Complementing the fitness centre are two squash courts, two tennis courts and a temperature-controlled swimming pool, set in a lush tropical garden area.

Overlooking the Gulf, the Holiday Inn Bahrain enjoys a prime location in Manama's diplomatic and business district.

The elegant frontage of the Bahrain Conference Centre.

The internationally renowned Bahrain Conference Centre offers stylish conference services, combined with the finest personal touch and state-of-the-art technical equipment. It consists of four multi-purpose banqueting and conference halls with a combined capacity for 1,600 persons, three executive boardrooms, four meeting rooms of varying sizes, a spacious pre-function area and lobby, and an elegant VIP reception lounge.

Famous for its seafood evenings, the Al Maharah Restaurant provides the perfect venue for fine dining.

LE ROYAL MERIDIEN

A leading resort in the Gulf for discerning travellers visiting Bahrain, Le Royal Meridien is ideally situated adjacent to the Bahrain International Exhibition Centre and just a few minutes from the Manama diplomatic and business district.

This five-star luxury resort hotel comprises 264 tastefully appointed guest rooms and suites, all fitted with the latest amenities. In addition, 43 Royal Club rooms are located on the sixth floor, where guests may take advantage of the exclusive services that include check-in desk and butler service.

With its reputed standard of excellence, Le Royal Meridien offers guests the choice of four sumptuous dining outlets; most notable is Nirvana, a gourmet restaurant serving classic Indian cuisine to the accompaniment of live music. Healthy snacks and light refreshments are available at both the indoor poolside bar and the outdoor poolside cafe. Live entertainment takes place every night in the Burlington Club and the Plantation Terrace.

Le Royal Meridien provides full secretarial service and technical support in its Business Centre; an auditorium with a 1,000 capacity; The Al Ghazal Ballroom which can accommodate 1,200 attendees, and has three multi-purpose conference rooms, all of these facilities combine to make business a pleasure for guests at the hotel.

In a subtropical setting of lush gardens and waterfalls, the Royal Sporting Club is the perfect place to keep fit or relax. A self-contained Hammam has a steam room, four pools and two massage rooms.

The Royal Sporting Club has an indoor pool with a tropical bar.

Each of the 264 guest rooms is unique, yet they share refined decor.

Le Royal Meridien is the only business hotel on Bahrain island with a private beach.

For the energetic, the facilities include a fitness centre, an indoor pool and a squash court. Within the grounds there lie a children's playground and tennis courts, with a choice of water sports on offer along the beachfront. Scuba-diving tuition is now available and includes a variety of underwater activities.

Continually striving to provide the height in luxury facilities, Le Royal Meridien has a new project under way, comprising a 26-berth marina; this impressive complex incorporates two docks with guest mooring and a portside restaurant. A further extension will accommodate a full-service boat-maintenance shop and cafeteria, each catering to boat crew's needs.

Finally, a spa – planned as the latest addition to the hotel – promises to pamper guests.

SHERATON BAHRAIN HOTEL

The Sheraton Hotel is centrally located between Manama's diplomatic and commercial areas.

The Sheraton offers a range of international cuisine.

Ideally situated between Manama's commercial and diplomatic areas, only 7.5 kilometres from the Bahrain International Airport and overlooking the turquoise waters of the Gulf, the Sheraton is one of Bahrain's premier five-star hotels.

Boasting 258 luxuriously appointed rooms, the Sheraton provides the perfect choice for both the business and leisure traveller and offers accommodation ranging from fully-equipped deluxe rooms through to stylish Junior Suites, and, for the ultimate in guest comfort, the Royal Suites.

Business travellers are specifically catered for on the executive floors where they can enjoy the services of a personal butler, make use of the fully-equipped business centre and partake of complimentary continental breakfast and evening cocktails in the Executive Lounge. The Executive staff can arrange courtesy airport transfer, speedy check-out and use of the Executive Meeting Room.

Since its opening in 1981, the Sheraton has enjoyed the reputation for the finest cuisine and dining services in Bahrain. With its extensive array of international and specialist restaurants and lounges, plus five-star quality banqueting and outside catering services, the Sheraton's position is established.

For the conference organiser, the Sheraton offers a wide range of banqueting room styles and sizes, all supported by experienced staff and the latest audio-visual equipment. The hotel anticipates the recently renovated Al Taj Ballroom becoming Bahrain's premier conference facility.

Leisure enthusiasts are fully catered for with the Sheraton's extensive recreational facilities, which include a temperature-controlled outdoor swimming-pool, two outdoor Jacuzzis, two flood-lit tennis courts, gymnasium, games room, squash court and health club with sauna.

With its blend of service excellence, fine cuisine and five-star facilities, the Sheraton Bahrain Hotel is the choice of both business and leisure travellers.

All the guest rooms are contemporary in style.

INDEX

Aali: p19,33,36,86
Abu Mahir: 56
Ain Adhari: p42,47
Ain Al Hunainiya: p81
Ain Al Safahiya: p93
Ain Qasari: p42
ALBA (aluminium smelter): p97,105
Al Fadhil Mosque: p45
Al Fateh Islamic Centre Grand Mosque: p47,51
Al Jaza'ir beach: p76
Al Hasa: p18
Al Khalifa: (family) p13,54,59,81,82;97
Al Mehza Mosque: p44
Al Seef: p19,69
American Mission Hospital: p11,44
Arad Bay: p55,91
Arad Fort: p57
Arabian Gulf University: p12,89
Areen wildlife park: p77,78
Assyrians: p17,21
Awali: p101
Bahrain University: p12
Bandar al Dar: p96
Bandar Club: p95
BAPCO: p10,75,97
Barbar: p18,62
Bab Al Bahrain: (Heritage Centre) p35,39; as gateway p44,
Belgrave, (Sir Charles): p100
Beit Al Quran: p51
Beni Jamra: p33,35,69
Bilad al Qadim: p18,42,44
Blunt, (Lady Anne): 84
Budaya Agricultural Research Station: p49,67
Budaya: p61,67,69,74
Burial Mounds: p13,15
Causeway: p16,53,72
Copper: p17
Crown Prince's Cup: p84
Dawhat al Muharraq: p53, 56
Dilmun: p7,8,10,17,18,20,21,22,27
Diraz: p33,62
Dhukan (see Jebel Dhukan): p8
Equestrian Centre: p67,84
Fishing: p29
Gilgamesh: p18,21
Hajjar: p21,66

Halat: p58,67
Hamad Town: p12,13,75,88,97
Hidd: p58,91
Holmes, (Major Frank): p9,10
Inzak: p18
Isa Town: p12,13,87,97
Jaaw: p36,97
Janabiya: p74
Jannussian: p66
Jasra: p35,69,72,75
Jazirat-al-Sheikh: p94
Jebel Dhukan: p8,81,97,99,103
Jidd Hafs: p35,67
Jidda: p73
Jufair: p39,91
Karbabad: p35,65
Kassite: p21
Khawkab Ash Shaikh: p93
Khor al Khaab: p93
Magan: p25
Manama: p8,11,35,38,41,61,84
Meluhha: p25
Mesopotamia: p17,25
Mina Sulman: p91,92
Muharraq: p8,11,35,38,53,84
Museum (Bahrain National): p22,51
Natural gas: p11
Nebuchadnezzar: p22
Oil: p9,11
Parthians: p22
Pearls: p11,19,22,27,100
Public gardens/parks: p47
Qanat: p71,72,74,75
Qal'at al Bahrain: p20,21,22,63,67,69
Qudaibiyah Palace: p46
Ras al Bar: p105
Reza: (Muhammad Zain al Ali) p11
Rifaa: p33,81
Sakhir palace: p100,101,102
Sakhir racecourse: p86
Sar: p16,19,72,74
Sargon of Akkad (King): p25
Sassanians: p22
Seleucids: p22
Shakhurah: p66,86
Shaikh Hamad bin Isa Al Khalifa: p82,88
Shaika Haya Al Khalifa: p22
Shaikh Isa bin Salman Al Khalifa:

p13,46,75
Shaikh Isa bin Ali Al Khalifa: p54,82,100
Shaikh Isa House: p54
Shaikh Ahmed Al Khalifa: p13
Sitra: p33,42,91,93,94
Siyadi House: p38,54
Souq Al Khamis: p42
Standard Oil: p10
Sulmaniya: Hospital p11,46; College of Medicine p12
Sumeria: p17,18,61,62
Tylos: p9,22,27,57,64,66
Umm as Sejour: p18,19,62
Umm Nassan: p73
University of Bahrain: p87
Zellaq: p75,76
Zuisidra: p18

PHOTO CREDITS

Aluminium Bahrain (ALBA): p90; p96 B; p97 B; Bahrain Promotions & Marketing Board: 80; 88 B; 98; Bahrain University: p89 T; Tony Cansell: p42 T; p49 B; p54 B; p60; Nazem Chouhfel: p12 M; p23 T; p26; p29 M, B; p65 B; Sheila Copson: p13 B; p30 T; p104 T; Chuck Grieve: p9 T; p10 B; p27 T; p42 T; p105 T; Rosalind Ingrams: p7; p10 T; p11; p16 B; p19 B; p20 T; p21; p24; p28; p29 T; p30 B; p31 T; p32; p34; p36 T, M; p38; p39; p40; p44 M, B; p45; p47 T, B; p48; p50; p51; p52; p55 B; p56; p57 T; p62; p64; p65 T; p66 B; p67 B; p68; p69 T; p70; p74 T; p76 T, B; p77 T; p79; p82; p83; p84 B; p85; p87 T; p94 M; p95; p101 T; p102; p105 B; p113; Ministry of Information, Bahrain: p14; p16 T; p17 T, B; p20 B; p22 T, B; p23 B; p42 T; p74 B; p75 T, p87 B; p92 T; p97 T; Shirley Kay: p8; p9 B; p12 T; p18; p19 T; p27 B; p31 B; p35; p36 B; p37; p43; p46; 49 T; p54 T; p55 T; p57 B; p58; p59; p63; p65 M; p66; p67 T; p69 B; p72; p75 B; p77 B; p78 B; p88 T; p89; p92 B; p93 T; p96 T; p100 B; p103; p104 M; Jim McEwan: p84 T; p86; p94 T, B; p100 T; p104 B.

*T: top   *M: middle   *B: bottom

THE AUTHOR

Shirley Kay and her family came to live in Bahrain in January 1968, on the very day Britain announced its withdrawal from the Gulf.

In Bahrain, the extraordinary sight of hundreds of thousands of ancient burial mounds fascinated Shirley, who spent much of her time documenting the antiquities, accompanying the Danish archaeologists, and helping refound the Bahrain Historical and Archaeological Society, of which she was the first secretary.

When she returned to the Gulf in 1985 Shirley was struck by the progress in Bahrain, which she had last visited in 1976.

Shirley Kay first moved to the Middle East in 1965, when she studied Arabic at Shemlan in Lebanon. Her youngest son was born in Bahrain in 1969. Shirley has lived in half a dozen Arab countries, about which she has written extensively in books, newspapers, magazines and for television.

Rosalind Ingrams who revised and prepared this new edition, came to live in Bahrain in 1996. Before that, she had spent many years in the Middle East.

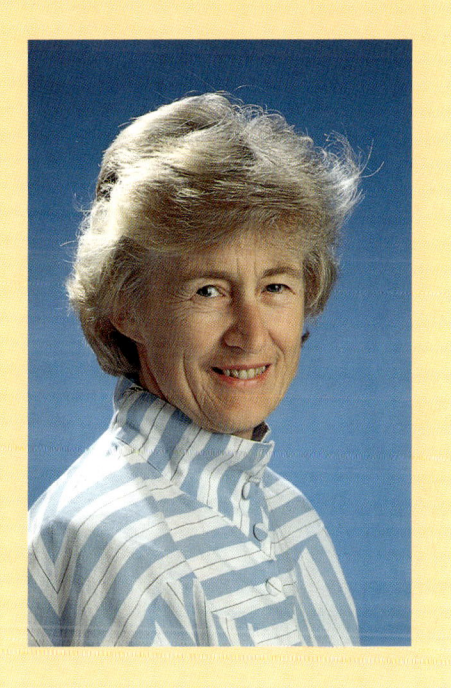

SELECTED BIBLIOGRAPHY

Al Khalifa, H & Rice, M: *Bahrain through the Ages*, volumes I & II, 1986
Al Muraikhi, Khalid, M: *Glimpses of Bahrain from its past*, 1991
Belgrave, C: *Personal Column*, 1960
Bent, J T and Mrs: *Southern Arabia*, 1900
Bibby, G: *Looking for Dilmun*, 1970
Crawford, Dr. H, Killick, Dr. R and Moon, Dr. J: *The Dilmun Temple at Sar*, 1997
Dilmun – the Journal of the Bahrain Historical and Archaeological Society
Frankfort, H: *The Art and Architecture of the Ancient Orient*, 1956
Izzard, M: *The Gulf, Arabia's Western Approaches*, 1979
Kervran, M: *Bahrain in the 16th century, an impregnable island*, 1988
Khuri, F: *Tribe and State in Bahrain*, 1980
Larsen, C E: *Life and land use in the Bahrain islands*, 1983
Lorimer, J G: *Gazetteer of the Persian Gulf, Oman and Central Arabia*, 1908-1915
Majed, Ebrahim Issa: *The traditional construction of early 20th century houses in Bahrain*, 1987
Oriental Press Manama: *Old Days*, 1986
Palgrave, W G: *Narrative of a year's journey through Central and Eastern Arabia*, 1866
Rice, M: *Dilmun Discovered*, 1983
Sandars, N K (editor): *The Epic of Gilgamesh* (Penguin Classics)
Walls, A G: *Arad Fort, Bahrain*, 1983
Ward, P: *Bahrain, a Travel Guide* (Oleander Press), 1993

ACKNOWLEDGEMENTS

The first edition of this book received generous help and support from HE Tariq Almoayed, then Minister of Information.

The author's good friend Samira Ali Reza provided generous hospitality, and guidance about the life of Bahrain.

In the new edition the author would like to thank Mohammad Ebrahim Al-Mutawa, Minister of Cabinet Affairs and Information, for providing the foreword. This edition owes debts to the kindness of many people, especially to HE Dr Abdullah Yatim, Undersecretary for Culture & National Heritage, and to the staff of the Library at the National Museum. Grateful acknowledgements are also due to Dr Pierre Lombard of the French Archaeological Mission to Bahrain, and to Drs Harriet Crawford, Robert Killick and Jane Moon of the London-Bahrain Archaeological Expedition.

Above all the author would like to express her gratitude to the Supreme Council of Tourism whose support and patronage have made possible the publication of this book.

THE ARABIAN HERITAGE SERIES

If you have enjoyed this book, you might like to know about some of the other Motivate titles.

COUNTRY GUIDES

Enchanting Oman
Bahrain - Island Heritage
Shirley Kay

Kuwait - A New Beginning
Gail Seery

Saudi Arabia - Profile of a Kingdom

UAE GUIDES

Dubai - Gateway to the Gulf

Abu Dhabi - Garden City of the Gulf
edited by Peter Hellyer and Ian Fairservice

Sharjah - Heritage and Progress
Portrait of Ras Al Khaimah
Land of the Emirates
Shirley Kay

Fujairah - An Arabian Jewel
Peter Hellyer

Al Ain - Oasis City
Peter Hellyer and Rosalind Buckton

NATURAL HISTORY AND CULTURE

Birds of the Southern Gulf
Dave Robinson and Adrian Chapman

Falconry and Birds of Prey in the Gulf
Dr David Remple and Christian Gross

The Living Seas
Frances Dipper and Tony Woodward

The Living Desert
Marycke Jongbloed

Wings Over the Gulf
Seafarers of the Gulf
Shirley Kay

Sketchbook Arabia
Margaret Henderson

Seashells of Eastern Arabia
S Peter Dance

Snorkelling and Diving in Oman
Rod Salm and Robert Baldwin

Beachcombers Guide to the Gulf
Tony Woodward

GUIDES

Off-Road in the Emirates
*Volumes 1 & 2,
Dariush Zandi*

Off-Road in Oman
Heiner Klein and Rebecca Brickson

Off-Road in the Hejaz
Patrick Pierard and Patrick Legros

The Green Guide to the Emirates
Marycke Jongbloed

PREMIER HARDBACKS

A Day Above the Emirates
A Day Above Oman
John Nowell

Forts of Oman
Walter Dinteman

The UAE - Formative Years
Ramesh Shukla

Dubai - A Pictorial Tour
Abu Dhabi - A Pictorial Tour

Yemen - A Pictorial Tour
Dr Scott Kennedy

UAE - Visions of Change
Dubai - Life and Times
Abu Dhabi - Life and Times
Noor Ali Rashid

THE THESIGER LIBRARY

Crossing the Sands
Desert, Marsh and Mountain
The Thesiger Collection
Arabian Sands
The Marsh Arabs
Visions of a Nomad
Wilfred Thesiger

ARABIAN ALBUMS

Dubai
Abu Dhabi
Sharjah and the North East
Shaikdoms
Travels to Oman
Ronald Codrai

*Further titles are available.
For a books catalogue,
call 971 4 824060 or
fax 971 4 824436.*

MOTIVATE PUBLISHING